NOT ANOTHER LASAGNA

How to Truly Help a Grieving Friend

**Bethany France and
Gwen Kapcia, LBSW, CT**

With love to Alek and Lindsey and:

Photo credit Bethany France

CONTENTS

FOREWORD BY CINDY BULTEMA

Life was not supposed to turn out this way.

After years of pain and purposelessness, things were finally looking up. My faith life was flourishing, I found my handsome prince, and was in the middle of planning my dream wedding. And then, with one phone call and the words, "I'm sorry, Cindy, David's been killed," everything changed.

My wedding notebook turned into a funeral planner, grooms-men were called to be pallbearers, and my fiance's parents and I sat shoulder to shoulder discussing favorite hymns, memories and who would make the ham salad.

As I rode with my mentor to the visitation, panic took over as I pictured myself standing next to my fiance's casket. Through a stream of tears, I whispered, "What in the world am I going to say to all of the people today?" My mentor lovingly reminded me, "Cindy, you don't have to worry about what you are going to say to them. At this moment everyone is wondering what in the world they will say to *you*."

That's the big dilemma, isn't it? Knowing how to respond when someone is faced with tragic loss is tricky. When there are no words, what is helpful to say? Not to say? What are you supposed to do?

How I wish the book *Not Another Lasagna: How to Truly Help a Grieving Friend* had been available during my loss. I would have passed it out by the truckload! What I personally discovered is although many of my friends and family members wanted to help, they didn't quite know how to. Thankfully, Bethany France and her co-author Gwen Kapcia give practical resources, suggestions and tips to help a hurting friend through this idea-filled book.

It's no surprise to me that God called Bethany to pen her story. Since first getting to know her almost ten years ago, I've watched Bethany walk through grief with courage, grace and vulnerability. I've witnessed her tackle the painful "firsts" associated with loss, and I've seen Bethany mark significant moments of remembrance with her family in creative ways. We've also celebrated—with confetti, of course—important personal milestones. Bethany has embraced both grief and gratitude while enduring the hard journey she will openly share throughout this book. And it's been my great joy to watch her live out 2 Corinthians 1:3-4 NIV:

> *Praise be to the God and Father of our Lord Jesus Christ, the Father of compassion and the God of all comfort, who comforts us in all our troubles, so that we can comfort those in any trouble with the comfort we ourselves receive from God.*

Cindy Bultema
GriefShare expert, Speaker and Author of *Red Hot Faith* and *Live Full, Walk Free*

INTRODUCTION

Most people want to skip reading the introduction, so I'll keep this short and sweet. First off, *Thank you*. Whether you are reading this book because your friend is grieving right now, you foresee a grief event for your friend coming soon, or you want to be prepared for whenever grief strikes, I applaud you. Grief support is not easy, but it is critical to help our friends feel loved, cared for, feel hopeful and be able to enjoy life again. I use the term "friends," but broadly it covers neighbors, co-workers, family and fellow community members – anyone that you have a desire to help. This book is laid out such that you can 1) understand where we, the authors, are coming from in terms of our grief experiences; 2) learn some facts about grief that might surprise you; 3) apply the tips and ideas pro- vided to put your talents and abilities into action; and 4) be inspired to not let your friend grieve alone. The first part of each chapter is written by Bethany and the latter part of the chapter is written by Gwen. We include our personal experiences as well as portions of stories from brave friends who were willing to share, correspond- ing bible verses (New International Version), Quick Tips (if you're in an urgent help-seeking mode, especially), and some additional questions or thoughts in each chapter to make the material more personal to you. There are references in the back for additional recommendations you can provide to your grieving friend. We hope you find this book practical, inspiring and with God's help, a blessing to your friend. ♥

Bethany and Gwen

CHAPTER ONE

HOW WE KNOW:
WHAT MAKES US EXPERTS
ON GRIEF SUPPORT?

· ·

The Lord is close to the brokenhearted and
rescues those who are crushed in spirit.
(Psalm 34:18)

In this verse above, it shows us that the Lord is never far from
those whose hearts are broken. He wants them to be rescued
and uses many means to do this, including our dearest friends.
By reading this book, you are or will be on someone's rescue
team. We are so glad you took the call to not just bring another
lasagna

· ·

Bethany

I never imagined that I would have, nor did I want to have, the expertise to write this book. What makes me an "expert" on how to help someone through grief and loss? I'll share a little of my story that didn't involve personal tragedy until my early thirties. I was lucky that I wasn't exposed to grief, but it also didn't prepare me to know how to help others get through losses. I, maybe like you, wanted to support friends but found it awkward, hard and was afraid I would say the wrong thing, so I often avoided those who were grieving.

At age thirty-three, with a two-year-old son, I came home from a routine day at the office to find my husband dead. Gone at thirty-seven years old. I was able to dial 911, remembered my neighbor's phone number and she quickly responded to the emergency dispatcher's request to come over and get my son out of his crib. Kevin always thought he would die at a younger age because he had a heart condition but certainly not dying in his thirties. He had endured procedures and different medications over the years as an adult, but atrial fibrillation was a treatable condition he tolerated. The cause of death was sudden cardiac arrest due to myocarditis (an enlarged heart). It was literally true that he had an abnormally large heart that, over time, just couldn't continue to work as hard as it had to keep him alive. Figuratively he had a large heart, too, as his friends and family can attest. It was, and still is, a huge loss for all of us. From that day, May 5, 2009, my world was changed, and my track of time became "before Kevin died" and "after Kevin died."

Having a two-year-old son, I chose to keep moving forward in a positive way. He and I needed to thrive despite the huge void in our lives. I vowed not to be bitter and sad but to make sure my little boy saw me as strong and resilient. I had experienced that people who have a grateful attitude live happier lives and I wanted that for my son and me. I attended support groups, seminars, and eventually led a support group for young widows. I reached out to new widows with helpful information and a listening ear.

I was lucky to have an amazing support circle around me including friends, family, and in time, a church family that changed my life. I had a best friend who didn't leave my side and called me just when I needed support. (Hint: if you feel a nudge to call your friend, do it. It could be God's way of using you to bring comfort, hope, or a laugh at the perfect moment.) There were people who stepped up to help in ways that made this hard road a little easier to navigate and made the horizon a little brighter. There were friends who helped with childcare, sent me notes and gift cards, and made me feel cared for in various ways.

I quickly realized even with all the support I had, there were still hurtful things said by well-intentioned people. There were awkward situations because it's hard to understand unless you've been there. My friend pointed this out during one of her consistent check-ins. She mentioned that she had bought and read several books on grief to try and understand what I was going through. Even still, the concept of how to help me (her grieving friend) was still a bit murky for her. At the next support group for widows that I attended, I mentioned that my friend had read grief books to try and understand my situation. In response, I received blank stares from some in the group while a few said, "Wow, that is a great friend." It seemed the other widows did not have people in their lives who took the additional step to really try and understand so they could take the appropriate actions. From that moment on, I was inspired to write a book for you—the friend of someone who is grieving so that you can be a blessing during your friend's tough journey.

What I found to be the most supportive ways of helping, things to say and not say, ideas for gifts, what to do when you unexpectedly run into a grieving person, how to be genuine in your offers to help – all of that is covered in this book. Your grieving friend will survive their loss, even thrive, with your help. Once you have a better understanding of what grief really looks like for your friend, what they truly need, and how you can help them, they will be blessed by what you've learned.

What Do I Have Against Lasagna?

Look, I like lasagna. My mother-in-law makes great lasagna. Please don't be upset because I hurt lasagna's feelings—or yours, if you've delivered this meal to a grieving person. It's okay if you have and continue to do so, but there are more options. Almost all grieving people I encountered mentioned receiving different versions or massive amounts of this pasta during their early grief journeys. While it's agreed that it was delicious, it earned the nickname "the death food" because it's what most people were provided with as a source of comfort following a death. This comfort can come with some downsides that you might not be aware of, but I'll get into that later. There are many other ways to help a grieving person, not limited to providing a meal.

Moving Forward

I was successfully moving forward after my husband Kevin's death, raising my son in our new normal of just he and I. It wasn't easy but we were doing it.

Fast forward three and a half years later, and I started dating a great guy and my life was filled with more smiles and laughter, and not as many tears. This man was well known with a great reputation in our community and beyond. After dating for a year, we went on a mission trip to Guatemala and he proposed, to which I responded, "*Sí!*" Four and a half months later, we were married.

Two months into our marriage, I had a pinch-me moment as we were on a tour bus of one of my favorite bands so my new husband could interview them. The lead singer said to my son, "Are you hungry? I can make you a PB&J!" My son gratefully accepted, and I was sitting back in awe at this life I was now living. My husband and I also had a secret that only a couple of close friends knew—I was pregnant. Later that night, while we listened to the band play outside under the stars, I looked at my husband and said, "I have everything I have always wanted. Our life is perfect." I was glad that my times of tragedy and loss were behind me.

But Wait, There's More!

Just twelve hours later, my new husband would be arrested for horrible crimes, plead guilty, and start serving a forty-year prison sentence. He had been living a secret, dangerous double life that shocked and damaged so many people.

Grief 2.0

Boom! There I was grieving again; this time, it was a figurative death. What I thought was true and good were dead, as were all the plans we had made. I was grieving the loss of a spouse that I loved and thought I knew. I was confused, angry, scared, frustrated, devastated, and sad for my son, who said, "Now I've lost two dads." I'd suffered through loss before, but this was a whole new level, with complications and added stress. I was ironically grateful to God for the first path of having been through and survived my loss of Kevin. That hard loss prepared me for, in some ways, the seemingly harder loss I faced with my second husband.

Once again, my support system showed up and kept showing up, caring for me and my son. Also, just as before, there were awkward situations, felt judgements, and well-intentioned, but hurtful, statements made to me. There were many nosey and personal questions which I didn't want to answer, nor did I necessarily have, or will ever have the answers. There were rumors and misinformation that I grew tired of correcting. There is still information that only I (and he) know. There were genuine offers of help that followed through, while there were offers of help that never materialized. There were friends that faded away, stepped back, or seemed to run in the other direction once I entered this new grief journey. There were also new friends made in the process and many unexpected blessings.

What this Grief 2.0 taught me, among many things, is that people around us are grieving for various reasons. Not just the physical death of a person, even though that is the most obvious. My new husband had not died, but my dreams and plans died with the discovery of the problems he had and his imprisonment. I was grieving the loss of a husband, a co-parent, and everything good I thought was going to happen with him in our lives. I was pregnant, going to the grocery store without a wedding ring on my finger, which made me feel insecure. I was grieving the stigma of living as a divorced person and the whispers and judgements that often accompany that. While my double-whammy situation might be unique, the feelings of loss and insecurity are shared with many who go through a divorce.

Divorced people are hurting and experiencing grief too. As I was involuntarily expanding my grief experience, I realized the need to expand our grief care. I looked at these figurative deaths in a whole new way. People who receive a devastating medical diagnosis for themselves, or a family member or friend are grieving, too. Their lives are now on a different path—maybe it's temporary or maybe it's permanent, and they are grieving the life they thought they were going to have. Parents or family members of someone who becomes incarcerated are grieving; the life of their family member is now different, maybe forever changed, and their lives as well are altered. Dreams are shattered. Learning to live a different life than what you thought and planned for is hard and sad and can be lonely.

While this book mainly focuses on how to help a grieving person due to a death, many of the ideas and concepts can be applied to other kinds of losses such as divorce, job loss, incarceration, and medical diagnosis. I'm begging you to consider those in your life, community, and workplace who are dealing with grief for any number of reasons. They need our compassion and care as well. Instead of judging and comparing the type and extent of the loss, we need to accept that they are grieving and start supporting them.

From "How I Know" to "Helping You Grow"

While I am no longer in the "thick" of grief, I am often reminded of it and can easily recall how hard it was to get through. But even with my experience, I find myself wanting to help others but being scared, too. Seeing our friends in pain is hard. I'd like to just "fix" their grief and see them happy again, even though I know this is not possible. God said "...in this world you will have trouble. ..." (John 16:33), so we all will face pain at some point ... or at several points in our lives. To really help our friends, we need to be willing to accept their grief without judgement and be willing to do the hard things. Grief is complicated and messy, but to have dedicated friends who are willing to truly "be there" makes the grief journey less isolating and more hopeful. Because of what I've gone through and who I've met along the way, I can help you learn how to be that supportive friend.

For believers in God, we are gifted in specific ways chosen just for us called spiritual gifts. In the Resource section at the back of this book, there are links to spiritual gift tests to help you discover them. Think about what you are passionate about, what you are good at, and what others say you are good at. Maybe you're trying to grow and help people in new ways. This book will help you discover the ways to help a grieving friend in the best way that you can. Maybe you don't make good lasagna—so don't make it. You don't have to make any food if it's not what you're best at. Maybe you wish there was another way to help, but you're just not sure what that is. Help is on the way.

Whether you are reading this book due to a recent tragic event for your friend, or you are in a position of wanting to be prepared and ready to serve when tragedy happens, thank you. Your desire to help is admirable. You can do this. Reach out, walk alongside, check-in, and follow through. Be there. You are appreciated.

Keep in mind—we are only human. You may find yourself admitting that your "go-to" phrases are the ones I recommend avoiding. Have you ever said, "Let me know if you need any-thing," to a grieving person? Me too! (Before *and* after my own losses). Don't feel bad—we've all said unhelpful things in hard and confusing times. We can all think of situations we wish we had handled better or friends we wish we would have helped more. But we can keep learning and trying; I know I still am.

Gwen

Hello, I am Gwen. It may sound odd, but I am passionate about walking beside the bereaved. I didn't know that would be part of my story when I sat in the 7-11 parking lot just weeks after earning my degree in social work and being newly married. I asked God to show me what He had for me to do. I boldly told Him that I knew He had a job for me. "Please take me to it, and I will do that job for you." We did not have GPS back then so when I became lost and needed directions, I stopped at a Hospice house and I remember thinking that hospice people are nice, and they can direct me where I need to go. After a brief conversation about who I was and what I was looking for (I thought it was for directions, but God knew what He was doing), I was offered a job as the bereavement coordinator right then and there. Since that time, over thirty-five years ago, I have become a certified thanatologist, which is the study of death, dying and bereavement and have remained passionate about helping the brokenhearted. But because I have walked alongside thousands of grieving people at the hardest times in their lives, I see and hear what they wish their friends knew.

I have created a guided tour through grief, written a Christ-centered curriculum for children, teens, and adults, and developed a Grief Mentor Training. I am a national speaker on grief topics and have been called into schools and workplaces after tragic losses. I offer stories from my lifelong career and what I have learned to be helpful to the bereaved. It is important to know that I have asked permission from each client for the stories I use, and I am deeply grateful that they have allowed their stories to be used to help others. For those who are afraid of being underqualified to help your grieving friend, I want to say this clearly: my credentials are helping to teach you, but you don't need to have my credentials or experience to help your grieving friend.

Don't sell yourself short—you can do this. God had for me a career; for you, He has you in the role of friend. If you have a desire to really help your grieving friend, that is your number one qualifier, your willingness! A heart that is ready to not only learn, listen, and follow through but to face awkward situations and stay where pain is present, is what is needed.

Last summer, I attended an outdoor Bible study that ladies from my church were hosting. I had not officially joined the group, but I happened to be riding my bike by the park where they were meeting. I was hesitant but felt the nudge to be uplifted and sup-ported by my sisters in Christ. The leader shared her devotion and then ended the formal gathering by playing a song. We all sat and listened as the words spoke to our hearts. A woman whom I'd never met, two chairs to my left, began sobbing. When the song was done, her daughter explained to the group that she was recently widowed and was in deep grief. I naturally turned toward her and began to ask about her story. The woman who was seated between us remained in her seat, appearing to be uncomfortable with this emotional discussion. I knew this woman next to me, next to the grieving lady; I knew she too had experienced heartache recently, as she was a recent cancer survivor. To include her, I asked if she could relate to some of the things this new friend was sharing. She did not respond; instead, she looked straight ahead and actually got up and left the circle a few minutes later. As I sat for over an hour listening to the widowed woman share, I could see my church friends giving me hand motions that they were praying for me as I supported this woman. That was nice of them; however, I was internally struggling. I was thinking, *What if I had not crashed this group tonight, who would have supported this new hurting lady? Why were all my friends so willing to let me, the perceived expert, handle it? Why did they not feel they could join in and contribute?* Fear? Feelings of inadequacy? Afraid it would spark pain in their own hearts? Yes, yes, and yes. I am sure all those were true, along with the thought of *Gwen is here; she can take care of it.*

How do I know this book is needed? Grievers need three things: to find the words, to say the words out loud, and to find someone who will listen to the words. With that knowledge, I want the women in the circle at the park, the people from my church and yours, and you the reader to be equipped to lean into the crying person, two chairs down, and listen to their words.

*What personal experiences have you
had with grief that help you understand
what it feels like?*

_____

_____

_____

_____

_____

_____

CHAPTER TWO

FEAR OF AWKWARD CONVERSATIONS: DON'T RUN, DON'T HIDE!

* *

Carry each other's burdens, and in this way,
you will fulfill the law of Christ.
(Galatians 6:2)

Loving one another (John. 13:34; Matthew 22:36–40) is one of Christ's commands. We can do this by "carrying each other's burdens" as well. We need to see other's burdens, listen, and look beyond the surface. These verses require two people; therefore, the challenge is to not avoid awkward situations and then to also realize that someday, we too may need to be carried.

* *

Bethany

Why are awkward situations common when it comes to interacting with grieving people?

- We unexpectedly encounter people going through a difficult time and don't have the "right" words ready.
- We don't know what the "right words" are.
- We don't want to bother them, add to their pain, or see them hurting.
- We aren't sure if they want to interact or prefer to be left alone.
- We, ourselves, don't want to think about a sad topic or a similar situation happening to us.
- We are busy and don't have, or want to make the time, to help.

Have you ever gone out shopping and really hoped you wouldn't run into someone you knew because of what you looked like or your lack of time to chat? We likely all have ... for a variety of reasons. Maybe you're wearing yoga pants that you meant to change out of before leaving the house. Maybe you have "bedhead hair/don't care" mindset until you do care and run into someone you know. Maybe you have a million things to get done today and think, *Please do not let me run into someone who wants to chit chat while deciding how I'm handling life based on my appearance.* What can also catch us off guard is if we see someone we feel like we should acknowledge but don't really want to at that moment. Maybe it is a friend that recently suffered a major loss, or you've heard is really struggling. Yikes. Should you approach them or not? Should you say anything, wave, smile, or just leave them alone? What would you even say? In times like these, you often must make a split-second decision. I am not always a quick thinker; later, I wish I had said or done something differently.

We especially don't want to run into anyone who will remind us we need to do more, do better, or make us feel guilty or sad about something. Most of us just want to get our items and get along with our normal and predictable day, not crossing paths with anyone that will interfere with that.

When a grieving person finally decides to venture out shopping (yes, it can take some time to brave the public scene), it can make them feel very vulnerable. They are trying to get back into a routine, preparing to see people they might know, and trying to put their best "I'm doing ok" face on, knowing they will be asked that question. It can be a pretty big accomplishment to get out the door and face the world that kept moving along when theirs stopped.

One of my first experiences out and about after being widowed was one I will never forget. I was slowly browsing items at a store and as I rounded one end of the aisle, my peripheral vision noticed a casual friend of mine looking over at me for several seconds. I was quite sure she recognized me but before I could acknowledge her, she put her head down and darted down another aisle. My first reaction was to wonder if she really saw me or realized it was me. I like to give the benefit of the doubt to people, but I know she did. I wonder if she just panicked, like I might naturally have done in her position.

My loss was so fresh, so I was guessing she either still felt bad for me and didn't know what to say, didn't want to ask me a dumb question (like how I was doing), didn't want to risk the chance of seeing me get teary-eyed or, worse, start crying. Or maybe she had previously said, "Let me know if you need anything," and hoped I wouldn't let her know right now, because she had a full schedule that day. I don't know. I'll never know for sure what her thoughts were that day. All I know is how it made me feel. Isolated. Sad.

You might think this was a rare occurrence with someone with whom I wasn't close, but it's common. In a 2017 survey conducted by the New York Life Foundation, about 63 percent of Americans surveyed admitted that they "have sometimes avoided talking to someone about their loss because they were worried they'd say the wrong thing."[1] People don't know what to say to a grieving person. They want to avoid feeling uncomfortable and sad, and generally want to avoid awkward situations. That avoidance tendency is natural since we don't want to think about death or loss as a real possibility for us or our loved ones, either. Thoughts that might go through our minds:

What do I talk about?

What if they start crying?

I don't want to say the wrong thing or make them upset.

What if they say they miss their person?

What if they see me buying a T-shirt for my daughter who's still alive and theirs isn't?

What if they ask me if I've seen their ex-spouse around town or if I continue to talk to them (in the case of a divorce)?

What if they talk about needing help with something? I am so busy!

I have no idea what to say.

I don't want to start crying myself; I'm still upset about the loss, too.

They look so disheveled—they clearly are having a hard time. I bet they want to be left alone.

---

[1] "New Survey on Childhood Grief Reveals Substantial 'Grief Gap,'" New York Life Foundation, November 15, 2017, https://www.newyorklife.com/newsroom/2017/parental-loss-survey.

My friend, Laura, whose son was undergoing treatment for a cancerous brain tumor, also experienced interactions where people were hesitant to say something, or avoided her altogether. Laura thought in her mind, *please just talk to us... My life isn't only cancer right now.* She would have welcomed conversations about normal life because sometimes she didn't want to talk about cancer. She had another child, a husband and all the normal life events and chaos that others have. However, she got the feeling that others didn't want to bother her with their problems because they thought she had too much going on or their problems were smaller in comparison to hers. She said she "wanted to be able to be supportive of other people and pray for them. It also normalizes life to know that other people are struggling, and it gives me the opportunity to support others and give back."[2]

Attending church can be a struggle for grieving people and also a source of awkward interactions. With my husband's funeral having been at the same church I was trying to attend now as a widow, I kept picturing the casket at the front of the church and where I said my final goodbye at the exit of the church. Additionally, that church did not have childcare during the service. As a single mom it was too difficult to focus while also keeping my toddler occupied. I decided to start attending a different church and loved it there. But once again, after my second tragedy, attending church was difficult.

Depending on the details of the loss, grieving people may feel like there's a spotlight on them so others can assess their well-being. These onlookers have two choices: to acknowledge or avoid. While a place of worship should be a supportive place, it can be the opposite because of the difficulty in understanding what a grieving person really needs. On the most basic level, be a comforter over an observer. Making eye contact, smiling, offering to sit with the

---

[2] Personal communication with author, December 3, 2022. Used with permission.

grieving person, and being willing to engage in conversation with them can make an impact on their desire to keep coming back to church.

Be aware that even if grieving people make it through the church doors, there could be triggers causing emotions to come out of nowhere. Worship music may induce tears or cause grieving people to walk or run out of the room. One song triggered for me such emotions I ended up crying in a bathroom stall for most of the service. I had memories from months prior of eating dinner with my ex-husband and members of that Christian band, who were asking about our upcoming wedding. Every Sunday, for months, I cried through the music. People next to me had probably seen my head down, my fingers constantly wiping my tears, and my swollen eyes after the service, but no one ever said a word to me.

Your grieving friend may feel uncomfortable attending church for different reasons than these but the important take away here is to offer to walk with them, sit with them, be ready to hand them a tissue or water or a shoulder to lean on. Offer to help with child-care during the service if that is an obstacle. Invite them to attend church services or events with you – offer to drive them there or meet them there.

School and sporting events are other arenas in which missing family members due to loss can cause awkward interactions. Getting the child to the event, cheering solo (again the empty seat next to them), not having that partner to share in the pride when your child succeeds, or helping with words of encouragement when needed can be a lot to juggle. If you see a single parent at a children's event, offer to take a photo of the parent with their child. Offer to help somehow, even carrying a chair or cheering on their child, too. No matter what the circumstance of why they are there without a spouse, think about how you can help.

One evening, I brought my new baby girl to an event at my son's elementary school. At this point, her father/my ex-husband had been incarcerated already for many months. Many people who were aware of my situation (it was quite public) had not yet seen the baby. I felt that spotlight of attention again – as if everyone's eyes were on us and almost no one dared to approach us. I had one friend come up to me and say, "Wow, she looks exactly like her dad. Wow," which was followed by awkward silence. What could I say at that moment? She was right; my daughter, especially as a baby, resembled her father. But I was already feeling so vulnerable and alone, seeing other moms and dads together at the school. I eventually replied to the person, "Yep. She does." I was shaky and didn't know what else to say. On one hand, I was grateful that she came over to talk to me. But I really wish she wouldn't have said that, not then, not ever. It wasn't a helpful comment to say to a single mom (of two now) who is dealing with postpartum and still grieving a hard situation with an ex-husband. I know this person to be a thoughtful and caring person, so I was not angry at her comment, but thought to myself, *why did she say this instead of just thinking it?* If you say something like this, catch yourself mid-sentence if you can, recover, and follow up with a better statement. Even if she would have added, "She's beautiful," or "It's so nice to see you here," it would have left less of a sad ending to our interaction. We talk later in the book about phrases to avoid saying and better ways to greet and comfort grieving people. But I felt it necessary to mention here that while I am encouraging you to acknowledge grieving people, be thoughtful. If you're caught off guard in seeing them, and say something that doesn't come out right, kind, or caring, be quick to apologize.

To say or not to say (something)

As the technology in our world has changed, having face-to-face conversations in general has become less common and more awkward. But technology has not yet allowed us to read minds either (perhaps a blessing). Since we don't know what a grieving person is thinking how do we know if they want to be left alone or actively cared for? Based on the experiences that I and others have shared, however, consider the impact on a grieving person seeing you dart into an aisle to avoid talking to them. If you see them, acknowledge them! At least say hello, wave, and stop to talk if you can. Ask how their day is going, ask how their kids or parents are, compliment them in some way—at minimum, say that you are glad to see them out and about, and hope they are doing okay. Let them know you've been thinking of them. Having suffered a loss can make a grieving person feel isolated – like no one understands their loss or maybe even cares. Everyone else returns to their lives and moves forward quickly, while a grieving person may feel like their world is turned upside down, and they are stuck in a state of sadness. To then add the impression that people are avoiding them can cause hurt, along with further isolation and confusion. I admire people who are hesitant and don't want to say the wrong thing, yet they go for it anyway. They err on the side of caring and acknowledging rather than avoidance. They put the other person's feelings before their own.

These acts acknowledge that the grieving person is seen, and there is a desire to care for them, even in seemingly little ways. People may appear like they are doing fine however, offer comfort anyway. Let them know if they change their mind and want company, want someone to sit next to, want someone to walk out to their car with them, or want some coffee, you're there to help.

And, *for the love*, when you see a mom carrying a baby, plus a carseat/carrier, diaper bag, and her purse down a flight of stairs … whether you know her story or not … offer to carry something. This happened to me, after church ended, while a family who knew my ex-husband extremely well and knew exactly what I'd been through watched me struggle at this and made no gesture to help.

I quickly learned not to expect such help, but it is certainly welcomed. Always err on the side of offering help.

Let's hear about some inspiring examples:

You might be familiar with the story of the Good Samaritan from Luke 10:25-37. This was a parable that Jesus told to an inquirer who wanted to know how to inherit eternal life. Jesus answered, "Love the Lord your God with all your heart and with all your soul and with all your strength and with all your mind; and, Love your neighbor as yourself." When asked for clarification on who exactly qualifies as "my neighbor," Jesus provided an example. One man was robbed, beaten, stripped of his clothes, and left for dead on the side of the road. (While a grieving person may not have these physical conditions, it certainly can feel this way emotionally). A "holy" person passed by this unfortunate soul, even crossing the road away from him to distance himself. A second person also crossed away from the battered person and continued on their way. But the third person, from Samaria (an unlikely source of kindness given the culture differences at that time) not only attended to him at that moment, but transported him to an inn, paid for his care, and said "when" he returned he would pay for any additional expenses. When others avoid the grieving person, even when it's awkward, be like the good Samaritan who cared for the hurting person.

Shortly after the second tragedy in my life, when I still felt many eyes upon me, it was time to drive my son to summer day camp. I dreaded it, in a way, but I wanted life to be as normal as possible for him, so I tried to keep the plans that we'd been looking forward to. When we arrived and entered the cafeteria check-in location, we expected to see a few familiar faces, but we didn't know everyone. I was relieved and hopeful that not everyone knew what I'd been through. A mom who I casually knew came directly over to me and, with a friendly greeting, expressed how happy she was to see us. She was warm, kind, and treated us as if things were "normal." It was surprising and refreshing, to say the least. I had figured if anyone dared to interact with me, it would be a tilt of the head and a sad expression, but probably no words spoken. Fortunately, this mom asked my son what he was looking forward to about camp that week. She proceeded to introduce me to her husband and another mom at camp who were also warm and friendly. It was oddly exciting, that I might not forever be known as "that lady who had that bad situation happen to her." I privately messaged that kind friend the following days and just thanked her for not treating me differently, like an outcast who had a spotlight on me due to my public tragedy. I thanked her for not avoiding me and just acting "normal" and sweet. You can have that positive impact on your grieving friends when you go out of your way to acknowledge and welcome them, no matter where you see them.

Including instead of avoiding & excluding

Besides a grieving person feeling avoided, they can also feel excluded. In many situations, there is a whole person that's no longer present: they are no longer occupying a space, a position, or a role. The grieving person has a void in his or her life, and it can result in them being excluded and uninvited from activities. In the case of a spousal loss, the grieving person is without their partner; "they" is no longer. This is hard on so many levels but for this chapter, I'll discuss the loss of couple-hood. The days of attending events for couples come to a screeching halt when someone loses their spouse. A grieving widow or widower can often feel left out from events, understandably so, on one hand since they aren't part of a "pair." They've already faced a huge loss in their life, and now the ripple effect of learning that they aren't invited to certain events because of their loss can sting even more. I'm not suggesting widows and widowers should be invited and encouraged to attend marriage retreats, obviously, but if you were involved with that couple before, think deeply about how you can still include the remaining person now. It's awkward, but maybe for an event with "pairs," you could offer to invite another single person (not matchmaking!) to be the fourth in your group. At least in the short term, be cognizant of showing too much physical affection with your spouse in front of a widow/widower because for some, that is a void that they may feel no one will ever be able to fill again. Try your best to include the grieving person without alienating them by thinking of activities where the focus is not on being a "couple."

Ever since Kevin and I were engaged, we spent New Year's Eve at a relative's house with other couples playing games. Apart from December 2006 when I had just given birth to our son, we never missed a year. After Kevin died, I was sad to think about missing this fun night, assuming I'd be an odd man out if I attended. Instead, these supportive cousins (on Kevin's side of the family nonetheless) kept the tradition going but added in other relatives and friends so that I wouldn't feel like the only person without a partner. A neighbor invited their single mother and sister; another friend was invited. It became a fun night instead of a couples' night.

A grieving person might not attend an event, but they want to be asked and included. It is possible that if you have friends who are couples, your relationships change with them. Remember, it's hard for everyone involved. The grieving person will learn which relationships will continue and which ones won't move forward with them because of the loss. But, as a helper to the grieving person, don't assume that because they are not a couple anymore, they're done with certain relationships or activities. It will look different, but it doesn't have to be the end of the friendship or connection. It's worth the effort in trying to maintain it.

My first summer as a widow, a neighborhood couple that we were friends with invited me to an outdoor show featuring a comedian. I was thrilled to be asked, quite honestly. I really liked this couple and enjoyed being with them. There were four tickets for this event, and their second daughter was not able to go at the last minute, so they asked me. It was perfect and felt good to get out and laugh, and they treated me to a great time. Did I think about my loss? Yes. Did I wish Kevin was there? Absolutely. Did I tear up once or twice? Yes. Am I so grateful I was invited, and I went? A hundred percent. Keep this in mind if you find yourself with an extra ticket—ask a single person who could use a night out without any pressure of it being a date-like setting. Or ask someone who is going through a hard time to go. They might say no, so give them permission and understanding to do so. Be aware that it could be hard for a grieving person to want to go out and have fun, and there might even be some sad moments within the fun for the person but ask anyway.

One inspiring bereaved mom, Tonya[3], took inclusion to the next level. Her daughter, Brookelyn, had passed away in an accident before entering the fifth grade but Tonya was watching Brookelyn's classmates now enjoy their high school senior-year activities. These were sad reminders that Brookelyn was not here to experience these milestones. She became aware of the need of two sisters who wanted to go to their prom but could not afford it since their mom recently passed away. Tonya raised money so the girls could buy dresses and get their nails done. What a great way to honor their mom by stepping in and making sure the girls were included in being able to attend the dance.

In anticipation of Tonya's own daughter's would-be commencement ceremony, Tonya reached out to other local bereaved parents who were likely going through the same emotions of not seeing

---

[3] Personal communication with author, December 1, 2022

their child walk across the stage that year. She sought their permission to have their child's name printed in the Commencement program's "In Memory Of" section to help preserve their memory for those that attended the ceremony. It is important to Tonya and to any grieving parent that they know their child is not forgotten and that a bereaved parent will always have a heart that won't fully heal. Whatever we can do to honor and remember our friends' loved one is appreciated.

Most of us, if we haven't suffered the loss of a child, can't imagine the pain that is involved. This is probably why it's hard for us to try and comfort a grieving parent; we are so sad for them and don't ever want to be in their situation, so we avoid contact. In doing so, though, we avoid caring for them or showing them compassion. With each milestone unrealized, with each changing season, the bereaved parent continues to grieve, so reach out often to a grieving parent. They appreciate it.

Gwen

When the socialization of the funeral is over and life is resuming, the pressure the bereaved feel to return to "normal" is immense. However, they are far from normal. They are changed forever, lost in a land of unfamiliar emotions, new roles, and readjustments that are never-ending. They are not sure how or who they are now. Experts say we need to slow down and turn inward. Go into neutral. Yet this is sometimes impossible because we still have to grocery shop, work, take care of children, go to church, etc. The bereaved risk going to these places and are all too often met with judgements, clichés, and insincerity, but the result is the same; they isolate themselves. "No one understands me." "I am just not ready to go out among people yet." They have many of the same fears as the helper/friend has about these awkward meeting situations. Friendships change, and others may even feel single people are in the way or feel threatened by them; therefore, for the bereaved, their circle of close friends must expand to bring the love and support they need. But this chapter is designed to help friends stay and understand what to do. Bereaved people have a heightened BS detector and can sniff out insincerity with alarming accuracy. We want the tools in this chapter, and the entire book for that matter, to relieve our fears and increase our effectiveness. Your willingness to approach them, to ask them, "How are you doing since your mother died?" "What kind of day is today for you?" and then remaining to hear their response, is important. Remember, you do not have to have the solution. This is not an "I need you to fix me," but more of "I need you to hear me."

Again, to ease your fears, to reduce the awkwardness, know that anything done with love and sincerity can be easily forgiven. We are not going to get it right all the time. But don't just walk away or avoid the interaction. If you walk away, it is another loss for the bereaved and then they carry what I call relationship pain. This is a pain they experience when people they thought would be for them have not followed through and abandoned them. Acknowledgment is key. Some people feel that by bringing up the loss, inquiring about how they are doing may remind them that their person died. They did not forget; they are always remembering and missing that person.

A man whose grown son had died and left behind a wife and young children was greeted at the coat rack at church by a fellow churchgoer and friend shortly after the death. He was asked, "How are you?" to which the bereaved man replied, "Well right now, I am somewhere between wanting to throw up or crying my eyes out. I am not sure which." Vivid. Real. Honest. But how to respond? Here are some ideas:

- "I am sorry. I can see how hard this is for you." Then be quiet and let them speak again.

- "I have never experienced this, but I can listen."
- "I do not have enough time right now, but can you meet for coffee on Tuesday? Or lunch on Wednesday?" (Be specific when leaving the conversation and when you are going to follow through)
- "I feel unqualified, but I would love to ask the prayer team to pray for you. Would that be okay? Or can I pray with you now?"
- "I would love to help you find support. Do you mind if I talk to (pastor, the care team, or other such person) about what resources are available and get back to you?"

In the example above, however, with the bereaved man at the coat rack, the typical, unfortunate response happened: the person awkwardly smiled and walked away. Sadly, the man who felt awkward has avoided the bereaved man ever since; resulting in relationship pain for the bereaved father.

Here is another example: a couple, whose wife works at their church, had a son who died. Returning to activities and church was particularly hard, so they decided to start by returning to their small group first. They entered, feeling awkward, but the group began with food as they normally would, then the study. As the group ended, the leader went around to ask for prayer requests. Their assumption was that maybe then they would be asked how they were doing; maybe then they could share their pain, and maybe they could be prayed for. But what is all too common happened. The group leader looked at them and, due to his fear, skipped right over them. Sadly, they have never returned to the group or to their church.

Notice both examples happened at church. We know the church is not made up of perfect people; however, we do assume or have a way of expecting more from our church friends. I think that is why it may cut so deep when we are hurt by church members.

As members of the body of Christ, we want to respond in a comforting, Christ-like way. When we can set aside our own feelings and temptations to avoid and bravely step in, show up, and share the love of Christ through our responses, God is pleased. His very nature is compassion. The Latin root of compassion is *pati*, which means to "suffer with."[4] Compassion is the ability to feel along with another person, the willingness to sympathize with the pain of a fellow human. It is what stirs us to act upon and help those who are suffering.

Maybe you can relate to those silent and awkward examples above. Or maybe you've heard or said something bolder in response to a bereaved person. I will give two bold examples, starting with the negative first. Three couples who attended the same church were close friends who raised their children together, attended graduations and weddings, and had that kind of friendship where they did life together. Every Sunday night after the evening service, they would go out for ice cream. The first woman to be widowed in the group returned to church, starting with the evening service because she knew it ended with her close friends being together. After the service, the other two women approached her and said, "It has been a great run, and we are going to miss you at ice cream." And just like that, she was cut out of a friendship. Now this widow was facing the loss of her spouse and her friends too, which was devastating, and you can imagine the relationship pain that it caused for her.

Acknowledge and maintain the relationship. I do not share this for shock value, and I assure you this example is not rare, sadly it happens all the time. If visitors were allowed in a support group, I would say go to one and hear it for yourself, but since this is not an option, you will have to trust me that I hear this often.

---

[4] Understanding the meaning of Compassion, compassion.com https://www.compassion. com/child-development/meaning-of-compassion/#:~:text=empathy,into%20the%20 realm%20of%20empathy.

On the contrary, this example shows two couples who met for dinner every other Friday night for years. The first woman widowed in her early sixties now felt so odd about going out to dinner with the other couple. I encouraged her to give it a try; maybe they could reduce it to meeting once a month, but she needed to see how it would go, and, after all, we need our friends. The night came for her first dinner alone with them, and they offered to pick her up. Upon arrival, the other woman jumped out of the front seat and went to the back seat of the car, to which the widowed woman was very uncomfortable and said, "Oh no, you ride in the front with your husband." Her friend replied, "No, I am sitting in the back with you." What a beautiful expression of love and concern.

Acknowledging. Doing something. Thinking about the event/experience from the hurting person's perspective and treating them with the same love and kindness you would want. What kind of friend do you want to be?

 **QUICK TIPS**

What not to do:

- Dart into an aisle like it's a foxhole and hope a grieving person didn't see you.
- Purposely avoid mentioning the loss or the person's name who died.
- Mention how tired they look.
- Suddenly look at your watch and say you "better get going," if the grieving person starts to open up to you or they get teary-eyed.
- Ask personal questions in a public place (finances, details surrounding the loss/manner in which they died).

- Blab on and on, complaining about something trivial in your life.

What to do:

- See them, acknowledge them, smile at them!
- Compliment them if it's natural to do so.
- Say that you are glad you ran into them.
- Tell them it's good to see them out and about.
- If they mention the person that died, acknowledge them, say their name!
- Ask how they are doing today, and specify that you mean today, at this moment or this week.
- Offer to pray for a specific need (sleep if they mention they are tired, stress relief, upcoming holidays).
- Offer to pray for them on the spot if it feels appropriate (but be ready for tears; it may happen).
- Offer a hug if you are comfortable doing so.
- Offer specific help if you can and follow up on the offer.
    Example: you offer to meet them for coffee and set a date then and there or follow up within forty-eight hours to set up a date. Maybe it is an offer that you've made before, but they haven't taken you up on it—offer again.
- Be genuine in whatever you talk about.
- Ask about other children/siblings, in the case of a child's death, and if there are any needs for the siblings that you can help with.
- Ask about anything else in the person's life—it doesn't have to be focused on their loss.

When was the last time you had an interaction with someone who is grieving? How did you initiate the conversation or respond? How will you interact the next time?

_____

_____

_____

_____

_____

_____

CHAPTER THREE

GRIEF: PHASES, ROADBLOCKS, AND JUDGMENTS – OH MY!

Do not judge, and you will not be judged. Do not condemn, and you will not be condemned. Forgive and you will be forgiven. Give, and it will be given to you. A good measure, pressed down, shaken together and running over, will be poured into your lap. For with the measure you use, it will be measured to you." (Luke 6:37-38)

Mother Teresa, widely accepted as a very wise soul, stated, "If you judge people, you have no time to love them." Oftentimes when we judge others, we do not have all the facts, so it is a simple solution to ask God to replace our judgments with love for His children.

Bethany

You didn't pick up this book to learn that "grief is hard." Duh. We wish there was a grief bandage we could help apply for quick healing, and yet, the thought of really trying to help our grieving friend can be as painful as ripping off a sticky bandage. We hate to see our friends in such pain, but how can we really help them? We ourselves may understand what grief looked like for us when we experienced it, but the circumstances are different for your friend. Or, maybe you haven't experienced grief on a major level at this point in your life. It's difficult to make the topic of grief a light read, so my goal is to make it a worthwhile one. Stay with me on this. While you aren't walking in your friend's shoes, you can still learn about what they are facing now and what might lie ahead. It is also important to understand and to be aware of challenges for us, as the helpers, that may be stopping us from being supportive. We will cover the so-called "phases" of grief, what grief really looks like, how we as friends tend to react, and our own roadblocks. Lastly, we tend to judge grieving people by witnessing their actions and decisions because we don't fully understand them. Once we understand more about grief, we'll save the judging for Judy.

Phases of Grief

I don't remember everything from high school, but for "some" reason (wink wink), I clearly remember when I learned about the "stages" of grief. (I'm a big believer that God prepares us for our roads ahead, even if we don't realize it at the time.) The lesson that day was about Elisabeth Kubler Ross's model that grief followed steps through the acronym, "DABDA," which stood for "Denial,

Anger, Bargaining, Depression, and Acceptance."[5] Since I had not experienced tragedy up to that point, I believed that those were phases that grieving people went through, in that order, and then the person was healed from their loss. I really wish the grief process was organized in that way.

DABDA may help us understand some of the stages grieving people go through. Let's start there but add in at least twenty-two more emotions. Then, instead of picturing an organized, linear, step-by-step process, picture a toddler's scribble fest on a paper. As the lines jet from side to side and up and down with no real recognition of shapes or order, this more accurately demonstrates a grieving person's emotions even within the same day. The grieving person is not crazy or rude – they are in recovery mode after a major loss. Remind them that you are here to support them, no matter which "stage" they are in at the moment or how many times they seem to fall backward.

Sympathy vs Empathy. If you're like me, I often forget the difference between these two words, but it is important. Expressing sympathy for someone is to say that you are sorry that they are experiencing pain or loss. This makes you an observer of their grief. To have empathy toward someone is having an ability to understand and feel what they are going through. To help your grieving friend in an empathetic way, it's important to understand the feelings of grief that they will go through, so you don't minimize their struggles, think they're crazy, or expect them to move through grief too quickly. If you have found comfort in Christ, you can share that feeling of comfort with your friend. In 2 Corinthians 1:3-5:

> Praise be to the God and Father of our Lord Jesus Christ,
> the Father of compassion and the God of all comfort, who

---

[5] Elisabeth Kubler Ross, *On Death and Dying* (New York: Macmillan, 1969). Elisabeth Kubler Ross, "5 Stages of Grief," accessed December 27, 2022, https://www.ekrfoundation.org/5-stages-of-grief/5-stages-grief.

comforts us in all our troubles, *so that we can comfort those in any trouble with the comfort we ourselves receive from God.* For just as we share abundantly in the sufferings of Christ, so also our comfort abounds through Christ.

Roadblocks to Helping

When it comes to roadblocks, if you're thinking that you are not capable of supporting your friend in certain ways, you might be facing some common obstacles. These include: knowing you can't fix it, comparing your abilities to others, fear, and feeling overwhelmed. We also might unintentionally judge our friend instead of really helping.

Maybe your reaction is like mine: when a friend has a problem, I am pretty sure I can find a way to fix it. Fixers usually have some connections, know a guy, or have ideas to offer. "Let's solve the problem and people will be happy again." That can be a functional mantra unless we are talking about grief, which we are. Darn. You can't fix or stop grief. Whatever situation has happened, it cannot go back to the way it was exactly. The moment they got the call, the police at their door, the serious conversation with the doctor, the papers presented, their world as they knew it changed. The new measurement of time becomes "before x happened; after x happened." This book is not a "Fix it and Forget it" model, so it's best to stop yourself from having those expectations now and to be more open to listening and understanding.

Comparison often hinders or prevents people from supporting their friend. Pastor Joe Wittwer of Life Center Church in Spokane, Washington, explains, "Some of us are prone to comparison unfavorably with others…. Stop worrying about what you don't have and start using what you do have."[6]

We see others use their gifts to support other people, and we conclude their gifts are better or more useful than ours. Your support can be just as meaningful as someone else's support that you perceive as more impactful. Don't assume since your grieving friend/ friends have others caring for them that they have all their needs met. You may bring the "something different," the needed gift that can build the mosaic of helpful servants for that person. Even a small gift or talent is still huge. Your heartfelt sentiment written on a card given to the grieving person, just when they needed it, could have an enormous, positive effect on them. A warm smile while looking them in the eyes, the filling of an empty seat beside them, kind words—go far. Grieving people need help and care from a variety of sources, because there are so many ways in which people can help them. Not only with meal service, but group support, spiritual counseling, practical needs (relating to housing, medical care, paperwork, yardwork, home repairs and improvements), prayer education, financial, and other ways. Try not to let comparison with others stop you from offering how God has led you to serve.

The other roadblock for not fully helping their grieving friends is fear. In the book *Discipleship Essentials* by Greg Ogden, three common fears prevent us from reaching out to those hurting: fear of failure, fear of commitment, and fear of confronting personal pain.[7] We don't want our efforts to backfire (fail) by making the grieving person feel worse or by saying or doing the wrong thing.

We fear commitment because what exactly are we signing up for? How is this going to affect my time and other obligations I

---

[6] Joe Wittwer, "Becoming Less: Use Your Gifts to Serve Others," sermon, Life Center, Spokane, WA, January 18, 2015, 12:13, 13:24, https://lifecenter.net/sermons/2015/ use-your-gifts-to-serve-others.

[7] Greg Ogden, *Discipleship Essentials: A Guide to Building Your Life in Christ*, rev. ed. (Downers Grove, IL: Intervarsity, 2018), p.179.

have? We can't say "yes" to everything because it means saying "no" to many other things, and we still need to take care of ourselves. If we are going to help, we want to do it well.

We fear confronting personal pain that might be brought back to the surface because of a similar experience for us, which we'd rather not revisit. We may unintentionally run away from the person to protect our own hearts. Even though I have a passion for helping grieving people, the thought of those heavy emotions returning to me makes me think twice about wanting to walk alongside them. However, it's worth it every time because it brings purpose to the pain. I, like everyone, am still a work in progress but we can be supportive with God's help. Pray for strength so you can be there for your friend. You can say, "Help me, God, to help them." Just know your grieving friend will appreciate you lifting them up and helping them stand. They also will be grateful for the other times when you sit down with them and do not force them to stand.

Pastor Joe Wittwer says about our fears, "Jesus is saying to us we have nothing to fear if you try. God is the one who has generously gifted you and God is the one who will handsomely reward any effort you make." He goes on to say, "The only way that you risk God's displeasure is if you simply refuse to do anything."[8] I understand the fear you may have; I pray that you find a way to still help your grieving friend. It might take creative thinking and expanding your willingness to help in ways you haven't thought of before – keep reading on! We will get to those other ways in later chapters.

It might be overwhelming to think about caring for your grieving friend for the long haul, especially when your friend has so many ups and downs. It can take an emotional toll on the supporting friend, too. You might see your friends and they seem like they are doing okay; they even laughed at your lame joke and agreed to

---

[8] Wittwer, "Becoming Less," 36:06, 36:20.

go out to dinner with you. Thank goodness they are back to their "old" self, you feel. But two days later, you check in again and they are having a really sad day. It's two steps forward, and three steps back with the grief process. Months can go by, and your friend is progressing well in their grief journey but a milestone event, holiday, a sign on the highway, or even a smell sets them back. They can experience several different extreme emotions all in one day. It can be draining as a friend to check in on them and see this progress go back and forth for months, even years. Seeing your friend in pain and going through some of those emotions with them is tough. I also want to point out that grieving people may lash out and say hurtful things to their friends who are trying to support them. While it can be understandable that they are not quite "themselves," it isn't acceptable for them to be verbally abusive. Should this happen to you, it may be a good time to step back and take a break for your own mental health. You can tell the grieving person in this case that you felt hurt by their comments, are trying to help, and need some space but will return when emotions have calmed. You can give grace but protect your heart as well. Ask God to give you what you need if it's rest or a re-fuel. Let your friend know that you're still thinking about them and will connect again in a few days or weeks, as appropriate. Even though you know truly being there for your friend is going to be hard, thank you for doing it anyway. From my own experience, I am so grateful for those who faced the hard task of walking along-side me even when they were tired, and I was emotional and "out of sorts." In turn, I will be there for them when they need me.

Judging vs understanding

It's natural to have your own opinions on what you might or might not do if you were in your grieving friend's shoes but be thankful that you're not. When you start to make judgements about what they are doing or the decisions they are making, it isn't helpful. When you hear yourself using, "they should" statements, it's time to pause and remember you are here to help them where they are at in the grieving process.

I agree with author Michelle Steinke-Baumgard, author of *Healthy Healing*, who believes that "We have done a major disservice to grievers." We expect them to move on. She writes, "We try to fit their grief journey into a linear path with arbitrary stages. We force them into unrealistic timelines. We don't give them the tools to start to feel better."[9]

Not only do we want them to quickly "get over" their grief and get off the emotional roller coaster, but we may also judge grieving people if they are not emotional enough. I am not generally a "hugger" or an outwardly emotional person. On the inside, I am very emotional but try not to show it—it's just who I am. Some may call it stoic while others might think that this personality style is cold. We all have varying levels of comfort with our emotions and physical embraces. There are several options to greet, say goodbye, and celebrate someone without close physical contact, if it makes someone uncomfortable for whatever reason. Sometimes going through grief changes this perspective, and sometimes it reinforces the way grieving people already are.

My own personal reaction to crises is to be that stoic person, to not show my emotion, and to appear strong and controlled. I was relieved to read in Michelle Steinke-Baumgard's book, *Healthy Healing*, that she acknowledged the differences in how people

---

[9]   Michelle Steinke-Baumgard, *Healthy Healing* (New York: HarperOne, 2017), Message to the reader, p.x.

grieved, and her "natural instinct was to be strong … and yes, distant."[10] This is exactly how I felt as well. Your grieving friend may wonder if their reaction and processing are normal, good, bad, typical, and unusual—it's not wrong or right—it's how they are. Let them react however they react. In some cases, depending on my current mood, if someone hugged me, it made me feel worse. The physical action of embrace, squeezing, closeness, and especially duration (if a long hug), and it could literally make me feel like I was crumbling and about to fall to the ground.

After my second tragedy, a close friend asked what I wanted from our group of friends. She said, "Is there anything you want me to tell them?" All I could think of was not to hug me. I knew it would be an instant sob fest and if I was feeling ok at that moment, I just wanted to keep being ok. Respect, and not judge, however your friend feels about affection. Now that I've frightened everyone I know into not hugging me the next time they see me, I want to clarify. Don't get me wrong: those that come in for a hug, I'll hug you—it's fine, really. I'll accept and reciprocate. But I'm not generally one to initiate a hug, and I firmly believe that is ok. Respect each other for their comfort level (whether they are actively grieving or not). Don't read into a lack of hugging as not being appreciative or being angry with you—it's just their preference, mood, or desire at that moment. We all deserve grace.

There are other people who thrive on hugs. That's okay, too. They might need that embrace. Asking if they could use a hug is an appropriate question, but don't be offended if they decline, even if you are surprised by that reaction.

---

[10] Steinke-Baumgard, *Healthy Healing*, p.5

The "inner six"

When I was going through my second tragedy, I was not sure who I could trust with sensitive details and/or who really needed to know. While I was, and still am, lucky to have a lot of close friends, I couldn't possibly (logistically or emotionally) retell certain things to several different people; it was exhausting. I established a small group of six individuals that I would call my "inner six," the people I needed most at that time to be my confidants and helpers when it came to details. Who would be in your inner six if you had to decide today? It probably depends on what the situation is, right? Your grieving friend may want you in their version of "inner six" but maybe they don't. It doesn't necessarily have to do with trust or closeness of friendships but boils down to what the grieving person feels they need; and that is not your place to decide.

After lots of thought, prayer, and counseling sessions, I decided to announce the news of my pregnancy via email to a group of thirty or so friends. I had prefaced the email with the exact disclosure that I was sorry I did not tell everyone personally; it was what I felt I needed to do at the time. I explained that I was emotionally exhausted and just couldn't handle telling each person individually, even though I wanted to. Plus, via email, I didn't get any sad looks, shocked faces, or follow-up questions for which I didn't have or didn't want to provide answers. I had one (now former) friend who responded to the email that she was surprised that she was told in this way, that she thought she should have been told sooner and personally. Instead of understanding, my friend made it about herself. We went back and forth via email a few times and then I gave up. She was not going to "get" it and accept my reasoning. We were never friends again. Please don't do this. Don't judge who the grieving person chooses to stay or become close to, or who they need to let go of. Even if you aren't in your friend's "inner circle," you can still be a huge support to them. They need you, too.

Another decision that is for grieving people to make is that they may find different hobbies or go on new adventures—eventually. Before my losses, I loved to travel. It took a little while after my losses happened to get that urge to travel again, but I was glad when it came back. Travel for me is a form of self-care, as the belly laughs I experience with my friends are good for my soul. About a year after my husband Kevin died, three friends and I journeyed to Ireland for ten days while my three-and-a-half-year-old son stayed at home with his grandparents. It took a lot of preparation, organization, and communication—but he was safe, and I knew he would be okay. The trip was full of laughs and extremely therapeutic for me in moving forward in my grief. Shortly after I returned home, I was ready to take off my wedding ring. (There's no time frame on that, either; just whenever it feels right for the grieving person.) Years later, someone questioned how I could have left my son at such a young age for that long. I felt the judgement of that statement as I reassured myself, "I'm a good mom." I'm thankful this person didn't say that before I took the trip, as I would have felt guilty the whole time or considered not going. This person really had no idea why the trip was so important and how healing it was. They had no idea of all the logistics that I planned to make this work—it's not like I just decided to go and left the next week without properly making sure my son and his grandparents had everything they needed without me.

Healthy Healing author Michelle Steinke-Baumgard writes that one of the ways she takes care of herself is fitness. She points out, "At a time when our lives have been shattered, we all need something that will pull us through. We all need a lifeline that will help us see the light again and help us find the strength to carry on."[11] For me, that lifeline is my faith in God but also time with friends and travel. Those precious times I'm able to travel for three

---

[11] Steinke-Baumgard, *Healthy Healing*, p.7

41

to five days (my usual trip length) give me something to look forward to and restores me. Without the willingness of my mom (and sometimes cousins and friends) to stay with my kids when I travel, I may not be able to do it. When your grieving friend learns what helps them work through their grief or find joy, be happy for them.

Post Grieving/The Next Chapter

Because there is no timeline on grief nor any manual for exactly how it should play out, let's agree we are all just trying to do our best. Grieving people want to keep going: they desire to pick up the pieces and survive and maybe even, someday, thrive. When you see people after some time has passed, they may appear that they have worked through their grief and are no longer "actively" grieving. That's wonderful. I pray whatever that timeline is for that person that they get to a place of peace, where they have more good days than bad, fewer breakdowns of sobbing, and more days of genuine laughter and happiness. There will always be moments, milestones, and occasional hard days where tears, even sobs, will return, but they usually will be fewer and farther between than they once were. Some people move faster than others and might start dating or make big changes.

One support group I attended had a focus one evening on the topic of hobbies. The leader said that his wife loved country music, and he hated it. But he listened to it because she enjoyed it. After she died, he switched to jazz. His friends thought, *Oh no, what is happening to him?* He also let his hair grow longer, started kayaking, and rediscovered what just "he" loved. Not right away, but at some point, your grieving friend may make lifestyle changes so just know it is part of the process of adjusting to their life now. Don't judge them for not staying the same or doing things that their person didn't like— sadly their person isn't here anymore. It's all part of the grief process, which is uniquely theirs. Please make sure that you, as the helper, aren't deciding when they should be done grieving, if they haven't grieved enough, or that they shouldn't change. It's not your call to make.

Gwen

Taking Off Your Glasses

A lemon is yellow, but if I look at it with blue glasses, I see it as green. Yet the lemon is not green; it is still yellow. I have so many things that influence the lens through which I see life. My lens (just like my prescription glasses) is individual to me. My family of origin, my culture, my belief systems, my Christian worldview, my past experiences with pain, and so much more have created the ways in which I see things in life. You are no different. To be truly helpful to your grieving friend, try to remember to take off your glasses, too. It helps to curb any judgement that may naturally start to distort your vision. When I arrive at the home of a client, or they enter my office, or in the waiting room of a Zoom meeting, I ask God to remove my lenses, allow me to be teachable and open to see what they see, and keep me from judging their responses.

If you have ever looked around this beautiful earth or if you have watched *Blue Planet* on the National Geographic channel, you know that our Creator is a magnificent artist. There are so many kinds of birds, so many colors of fish, and multiple shapes of terrain on this earth. The variety is amazing, and we see that same variety in humans. How we look, how we feel, how we react. Therefore, there is a vast variety of how we grieve, and no right or wrong way to experience grief or trauma.

As a friend to a bereaved person, we need to do a few things after we remove our lenses. First is to familiarize ourselves with common reactions to loss. There are physical reactions, such as body retardation that occurs where the person experiences a lethargy that requires much rest because of grief. Some experience tightness of the throat or heaviness of the chest. The inability to concentrate is common as well. Feeling guilty, sensing your person's presence, even expecting them to walk through the door or hearing their voice can happen often.

Assuming mannerisms or traits of the deceased, feeling anger, or having mood changes over the slightest things is also common. If I were to sum up reactions that I want you as a friend to know, it is this: grief is a lack of understanding and a loss of control, and the griever has no idea what to expect, so most bereaved feel as if they are certainly going "crazy."

Secondly is to understand their story, which in turn affects their response. There are many things that factor in here, so here are a few: who was this person to them? What role did they play in their life? What is the unique personality of the griever and the deceased? What other stressors are in their life at the same time, such as health problems, financial issues, etc.? The age of the person who died, the circumstances surrounding the death, and if they experienced multiple losses are also varying factors.

It would behoove us to take a teachable posture with our grieving friend. Our understanding is that they are going to react differently than we do and that in this overwhelming complex time of need, they are literally "torn apart," which is what the word bereaved means. The up and down of mourning is that it is a process in which we are all over the place; there is nothing systematic about it. There is no quick fix, as it can be tolerable one moment and unbearable the next. We, as their friends and family, need to be sure we are not locked into a set time frame or rhythm of what their journey is to look like. The best gift we can give is to allow them to feel, express, and react in the way they need to. Ask God to give you eyes to see and ears to hear how they are affected by this pain and help them celebrate their own uniqueness.

Can we just take a pause here and thank God that He created us all special and unique? Wouldn't life be boring if we were all the same?

The odd thing about grief is that we all have this idea that we know what it feels like and how it plays out——until it happens to us. We come to realize that there is no set way to grieve. We learn it is deeper, harder, and tears us apart in ways we never even imagined.

Here are four conventional thoughts in our society about grief and mourning:

- It should be short-lived: "Aren't you over this yet?" "Stop moping around." There is pressure for the grieving person to heal quickly and get back to "normal"
- It is experienced linearly: grieving is the most unpredictable, upside down, chaotic experience. There is no magical end. There are no stages.
  - Referenced above is the concept of DABDA, introduced in 1969 by Elizabeth Kubler-Ross, author of *On Death and Dying*. It's really important to note that in the updated, 40th-anniversary edition completed in 2010, Allan Kellehear PhD, a medical and public health sociologist, clarified in the introduction, "*On Death and Dying* was never a study of grief and bereavement. It was a discussion of some key emotional reactions to the experience of dying. Yes, grief was a part of that experience, but it was not the totality of the experience."[12] Some clinicians and lay persons are still using the old thoughts and time frames for grief, therefore keeping bereaved people with a false notion that they can flow through grief in an orderly fashion.

---

[12] Allan Kellehear, introduction to *On Death and Dying*, by Elisabeth Kübler-Ross, 40th anniversary ed. (Abingdon, UK: Routledge, 2009), viii.

- That there is closure or that it is recoverable: myth that there is closure, when it's a lifetime membership. There is no cure, but we do heal. Our life will always be flavored by the loss. The wound will heal, but a scar remains, and many times we bump the wound, and it hurts all over again.
- Fixed Rationally: there is no pecking order as to what grief hurts worse; it is not fixed by the label they wear. Some examples of labels I have heard from my clients' experience are: "He was just your uncle," "You can have other kids," or "You are young; you can get remarried."

Why do we feel that we know what is the proper way to grieve or the right amount of time? Do we have a set of beliefs about grief, and is our thinking getting in the way? We can get our feelings hurt when a bereaved friend isolates for a while. We can take that personally rather than realizing they're in a whirlwind of grief, trying to figure out and make sense of their world now, and it is not for us to be offended or to judge. I recently had a friend express that she was upset with a grieving friend of hers for seeming to not have any interest in (my friend's) life. I had to ever so gently say, "It is not about you. Her whole world is upside down, she has no idea who she is now without her husband; she is not worried about how you feel or what is happening in your life. Please be patient with her."

Gender-Based Judgment

We put expectations on men, especially, to be self-sustaining. Meaning, we make it harder for them to ask for and to accept help. We expect that they are the strong caretakers of the family and to hold it together. The thought that "men/boys do not cry" is more of an old-fashioned notion but one that still is carried on in some families. Men are created differently than women and express emotions differently, but it does not mean that they do not hurt. I was asked to go to the home of a couple whose young daughter had died. When I arrived, the wife was so visibly mad, telling me that her husband was not joining our visit because he was not grieving. As we walked to the living room, and passed by a window, I saw him in the backyard chopping the biggest pile of wood I had ever seen. The wife stated, "That is all he has done since she died." I gently nodded and replied, "That is a lot of grief in your yard." She had been judging him and thinking he was not grieving because he wasn't crying in the same way she was. When she could see his physical response as his expression of grief, it was a game-changer. This made her see his grief process in a new and compassionate way, even if it wasn't the same way she was expressing it.

For spousal loss, women tend to redecorate after their spouse dies, and it seems many judgments are made—that it is too soon, or not the right thing to focus on. But generally, are not women the keepers of the nest? Do we not put our homes together, so all are comfortable? Some women do not change a thing in their home—neither is wrong. Men, generally, are quicker to find a new partner if they become widowed, while women who become widowed tend to wait longer. There can be many explanations for this, but the important takeaway is to not judge the length of time it takes to find a new mate, or if they even consider that possibility. Too much emphasis is put on the differences between genders and not enough on the capacity to grieve, mourn, and move forward.

Faith-Based Judgements

All too often, our judgments come because of our spiritual beliefs, and we look cross-eyed at someone's apparent lack of faith or if they dare to be angry at God. Remember that God understands our pain. When a friend seems to believe God has no interest in their life since this painful event, or has deserted them or is punishing them, the friend needs to know that the loss did not change or move God: He is still there. He is still loving and still caring. He has patience and allows for His children to kick and scream if they need to, all the while He holds us in His arms to comfort them. It will only make things worse if we condemn our brothers and sisters during this time; God does not need us to defend Him. He needs us to walk alongside our friends and listen in love. If your friend is challenging God, you can reassure them but understand that God is working in their hearts, too, and it may take time.

Try not to allow your beliefs to get in the way of helping others either. The ACES study, which stands for Adverse Childhood Experiences, has principles to best prevent the long-term effects of ACEs.[13] Basically, instead of looking at a child and saying, "What is wrong with you?" they say, "What happened to you?" When I studied that, I realized Jesus is the original creator of that concept. The most helpful position we can take is to dethrone our ideas/judgments as the only right ones, and to remove our lenses and look at them from the grieving person's viewpoint.

You may not understand how your friends are reacting to their pain and you may not approve. But decide if you can help regardless. And keep the judging to Judy!

---

[13] https://www.cdc.gov/violenceprevention/aces/index.html CDC-Kaiser Permanente Study 1995

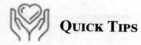

Quick Tips

- Grief is not a linear process – setbacks are common and expected. Grieving people experience many emotions often at unexpected times.
- You, as the caring friend, may have roadblocks to helping. While understandable, you can overcome them and be the supportive friend you want to be.
- Seek to understand so you are not apt to judge.
- Avoid using the word "should" in the context of what you feel they aren't doing right.
- Don't imagine what you would do in their situation and impose your displeasure on them.
- Remember that their manner of, and timing of, grieving is not up for grading.
- Remind yourself that you are not in their shoes, even if you've experienced loss or death.
- Be supportive, caring, and patient without your opinion expressed.

Think about a few people that you have known who have been through grief. How did they handle it differently from each other? Do you think you unintentionally placed judgements on any of them for how they dealt with it? Ready to remove your glasses?

CHAPTER FOUR

JUST BE THERE— LET PRESENCE BE YOUR GIFT

• •

"He says, Be still and know that I am God." (Psalm 46:10)

The Hebrew word for "still" that's used in Psalm 46:10 is *raphah*, which means to "sink down, relax, let go, cease striving, or withdraw."[14] Remember the context of this verse: its context is during the time of conflict of war. We are asked to stop our efforts and not try to solve things that are in God's domain. Where we can stand in awe of His mighty power and just be.

• •

---

14 "The REAL Meaning of Be Still and Know That I am God – Psalm
    46:10," Jeffrey Curtis Poor. April 25, 2022. https://www.rethinknow.org/
    psalm-46-10-meaning-of-be-still-and-know-that-i-am-god/

Bethany

The shortest and most simple-sounding advice I can offer you is "Just be there." Remember, a grieving person can feel isolated, confused, sad, lost, angry, depressed—sometimes all at the same time. They are in a daze; they are anxious; they are forgetful; and they can't help it. Sometimes they want to be busy and surrounded by people. Other times they want to be left alone. In Michelle Steinke-Baumgard's book, *Healthy Healing*, she explains, "I couldn't tell you which was worse, being alone or being surrounded, because ultimately I was just deeply and painfully lonely."[15] Even if grieving people are not sure what they want now—to be with someone or not—they always want to know that someone cares for them. The better advice is to "be there" rather than not. You will not take away their loneliness, but they will feel your love and care for them when you are present with them.

Don't assume that the grieving person has who they need with them. Families are complicated. Even a large family or seemingly close family may not be as supportive of one another as friends or those beyond their inner circle. You might think that because they have several siblings, they are supporting each other, and you don't want to interfere. But you shouldn't assume the dynamics of the family mean they are providing the needed support. Don't be afraid to show up and stay regardless of how their support system appears.

I am a big fan of the Christian music genre and there are many songs that have spoken directly to my heart in times of sadness and times of praise. It helps to be still and focus on the lyrics. Because I am familiar with Christian music, I will often text a hurting friend and include a link to a song. When I can't find the words, I let music

---

[15] Michelle Steinke-Baumgard, *Healthy Healing* (New York: Harper One, 2017), p.139

speak for me. In following these talented artists, I've learned more about their stories and have shared a few examples in this chapter.

Just Be There for Men Too

One morning, a Christian radio station featured an interview with a popular male singer/songwriter, Jason Gray, where he was asked about how he made it through a difficult time in his life recently. He recalled a night on his tour bus, in between concerts consisting of entertainment, praising God, and bringing hope to his listeners. What his fans didn't know was the immense grief he was facing in his personal life. He and his wife of a few decades were going through the process of divorce. Anyone in the public eye, especially in the Christian music industry, can face scrutiny for their decisions, and divorce is never an optimal choice. This performer was tired and grieving the inevitable outcome of the death of his marriage. He was on his tour bus where he hoped to unwind with a close friend. He could sense the friend was going to do what others did, offer him some advice about his impending divorce. Maybe he would express his disappointment or try to offer some ninth inning fixes that he heard several times before.

Instead, the friend asked if he could give him a hug (cue the awkward silence for a few seconds). He somewhat reluctantly agreed. His friend hugged him with such force that the hesitant recipient almost lost his footing. But his friend didn't let go. The bear hug kept going, past the awkward ten seconds and now, with no end in sight. Strangely and slowly, he felt himself start sobbing. Not just tears welling up, but ugly crying that most people are afraid to do in front of anyone. No words were said during this time. After several minutes, he finally took a deep breath, and both men collapsed into opposing cushy chairs. He recalled the scene as one of the most powerful and helpful things any friend had ever done for him. No judgment, no advice from someone not walking in his shoes, no probing personal questions: just being there with a hug. He later released the song, "Death Without a Funeral," which describes this type of grief.[16]

In another example, "Not saying anything" musician Ben Calhoun agrees, "was more helpful than saying just something to fill the air."[17] Ben is from the Christian music group Citizen Way and had mentioned during a concert that he went through the hardest time in his marriage about six months prior. His wife had suffered a miscarriage, and it was an extremely tough time. Just being present with the hurting is an important and valued gesture. He refers to Romans 12:15: "Rejoice with those who rejoice; Mourn with those who mourn."

There seems to be a stigma, especially with men, about being emotional in public, so attempting to comfort grieving men can seem tricky. Offering to meet for coffee or listening to how they are really doing, without offering a fix, is valuable to a grieving man, even if they don't look like they are grieving.

Just Bring Coffee

Laura Story, musician and author of *When God Doesn't Fix it*, recalls being by the bedside of her husband who was fighting a brain tumor. For months, the outcome was uncertain, and Laura was tired and scared. They had only been married a short time and had big dreams in their lives. Living far from family, canceling her husband's schooling (and potentially his long-term career plans), and not understanding God's plan were unexpected detours that

---

[16] Jason Gry/Andy Gullahorn, "Death Without a Funeral," track #7, on "Where the Light Gets In," Centricity Music, 2016, Compact Disc.

[17] Ben Calhoun (lead singer and guitarist, Citizen Way), personal interview with Bethany France, October 13, 2016, Kentwood Community Church, Kentwood, MI.

sent Laura into grief. Her husband had been athletic and healthy; now he was sick and helpless. Many months were spent at the hospital, many tests, predictions from doctors and ever-changing conditions made Laura's journey more difficult than she ever imagined her life would be. Amid one of her lengthy hospital visits, she recalled a friend entering the hospital room and handing her a coffee, saying, "Here's your latte." She didn't try to fix it, offer advice, or try to direct Laura's actions. She didn't offer scripture, which wasn't always helpful to Laura during this time in her life. She just sat beside her and was there.[18] Most people, even grieving people, won't turn down a drink when it's brought to them. They might have a problem asking someone to go get them a drink or responding with a request for one if someone asks if they need anything. But if you just bring them one, they aren't likely to refuse it.

Just Be There at the Visitation/Funeral

If you are very close to the grieving person, you might be called to their home the same day as the loss, or in the immediate days after. If you are not called to their side that quickly, the process of you being there may start with the visitation in a funeral home. This is never easy and makes many people uncomfortable, with some avoiding viewings/funerals altogether.

I have overheard people say they wanted to attend a funeral, but they just hate those sorts of things. (As opposed to some other people, who enjoy funerals? Come on.) After all, what if you see someone crying? It is very upsetting to see people, especially friends or family, in such pain. Generally, we want to avoid doing upsetting things because what if their sadness makes you break down? What if attending these events makes you start wondering

---

[18] Laura Story, *When God Doesn't Fix It* (Nashville: W Publishing, 2016), p.53.

if this could happen to you or your child/spouse/parent? That might envoke great anxiety and fear in you. God forbid this ever happens to you, but remember it *did* happen to the grieving person, and there's no changing it now.

Here are some reasons you might have for not going to a funeral or staying long. Maybe you didn't know the deceased person that well. After all, the grieving person probably won't even remember if you were there or not. Plus, look at that line out the door, of people waiting to give their condolences … it's probably best if you just post an endearing comment on social media (sarcasm and disappointment inserted here). I still struggle with making myself go to funerals and visitations because it is so difficult, but I remind myself that this is not about me—it's for the support of the grieving.

You may get the opportunity to be the Naomi to your friend Ruth. The story of these two women is one of grief but also dedication and support despite a hard situation. Naomi was married and had two sons, one of whom married a woman named Ruth. After both of their husbands died, Naomi encouraged Ruth to go back to her hometown as Naomi returned to hers. Ruth said (in today's equivalent language), "Nah. I'm good. I'm staying with you." Naomi urged her again to go back home, not expecting anyone to stay with her and take care of her. But Ruth replied, "Don't urge me to leave you or to turn back from you. Where you go I will go, and where you stay I will stay. Your people will be my people and your God my God" (Ruth 1:16). I'm not suggesting you move into your friend's house and forget about your own family, but you can show your friend you're there to stay as long as she or he needs you and then some. As with the case of Ruth and Naomi, you may experience unanticipated blessings for your dedication.

My friend, Joly, aka my "Ruth," rushed to my side when she heard the news of my husband's death, driving several hours from her home to our home. She stood beside me during the four long hours of viewings and never left me unless she ran to get me water or more tissues or anything that I needed. She literally never left my side. As I continued to cry and greet everyone who came in, repeating the story hundreds of times, her eyes welled up continuously. She wasn't afraid of the pain—from her tired feet to her empathetic heartache. She didn't care if she was exhausted or had never met most of these people who were coming to console me. If there was an awkward silence, she filled it appropriately; but if there was just silence between two heartbroken friends, she knew she didn't need to fill it—she knew to just be there. Her constant presence was such a comfort to me. Years later, she would rush to my side after my second tragedy, this time bringing her newborn with her. She stayed with me and oversaw phone calls and visitors and whatever else I needed. Don't shy away from being this dedicated support in the hardest days of your friend's grief.

I would encourage you to listen to the song by Nichole Nordeman and Amy Grant, "I'm With You,"[19] which was inspired by Ruth & Naomi and may inspire you to make sure your friend knows you'll be there: physically, emotionally, however long they need you to be. God cares for the grieving many times through friends like you who will be there and stay. Anyone else who witnesses your kindness of being there will hopefully be inspired to do the same.

Silence is Golden

A grieving person has so much to do. There is often chaos, incoming phone calls and outgoing phone calls to be made, doorbells ringing to respond to, and personal questions to screen, so life gets loud. By not contributing to the noise, by not feeling like you have to say something profound or even just comforting to a

---

[19] Nicole Nordeman & Amy Grant, "I'm With You," track #7 on The Story, EMI Christian Music Group, 2011, compact disc.

grieving person, you are allowing some peace to surround them, even for a few minutes.

The Bible gives us an example from a man named Job who suffered unimaginable losses and was left with nothing. Three of his friends, upon hearing of his suffering, came to see him. Eliphaz, Bildad, and Zophar traveled to console Job with seemingly good intentions. They wept for his suffering and sat silently in Job's presence for seven days, which was tradition. This all seems like Job really had great support from these friends—way to go, guys, fist bump! However, the story took a nasty detour when the friends decided that it was time to lecture Job on the reasons they believed he was suffering. Oh boy. They explained that they believed his suffering was brought on by his own actions— ouch. Job responded, eventually, in 13:5 by saying, "If only you would be altogether silent! For you, that would be wisdom." He continues in chapter 16, "you are all miserable comforters." What started out as a support system turned into making Job suffer even more. It also seemed that they felt his suffering had gone on long enough. When we try to rush our friends through their grief or get tired of . hearing them talk about the person who died or their story, we are miserable comforters. Just being there for him in silence was more helpful for Job.

Be There but Also Be Aware

There are exceptions to the rule of "just being there," and it is possible to wear out your welcome. Be on the lookout for any hints that your time to leave or step back has arrived and be respectful that sometimes a grieving person wants to be alone, or maybe you are not that person that they want standing next to them all day. Do not be offended here, people. It is not about you; it is about what the grieving person needs in that moment of time. If you sense, or the person flat-out states, that they are ok without you there, respect that. You can try to help them again later, but don't be too pushy or you may push them away for good. Be ready to jump back in if they indicate they want your help. Give the grieving person permission and an easy way to tell you that they need some space during their grief.

Please be patient and understanding with the grieving person. Whether you are an in-law, out-law, neighbor, co-worker, best friend, mom, sister, or long-lost pen pal, let the grieving person direct who they want by their side and try not to comment about it or be hurt about it. Continue to be supportive regardless of what role you think you should be playing in their life. Tragedy changes relationships in many cases and knocks routines out of whack. Schedules and even friendships might be different for a while, but don't give up on your support. Love the grieving person as much as you can without any other agenda than to be helpful.

It's important to listen without interruption to a grieving person. Whether the grieving situation was sudden or expected, there can be shock and disbelief by the one left standing. Situations and conversations are played repeatedly in their mind. There are self-directed questions such as, "If only I'd …" that make the grieving person question their actions and make grieving more complicated. However, it is not your job or place to know these answers. Some of the most helpful actions you can provide are to just listen and not say anything. Let the grieving person recount, replay, remember, and retell. Know that when you make quick suggestions, you might be inadvertently confirming their fears that they should have done something to prevent this tragedy from happening.

The fact is, sometimes there are no answers. At least, we won't know the answers this side of Heaven. It is ok to tell your loved one or friend any of the following responses if you feel being silent isn't the best option:

"I wish I had answers for you…"
"It's so hard to understand why…"
"I can see why you have these questions, I would (or do) too…"

Just remember, being quiet but present is perfectly ok.

Gwen

Close your eyes and recall someone who showed you great compassion. Hold them in your thoughts for a moment while you allow yourself to remember what it felt like to be in their presence. Now go and be that person for your friend who is grieving. It isn't someone's words we recall; it is their presence and how they made us feel.

First, please put your electronics away. Being on your phone when in the mourner's presence gives the message that what they share is not important to us. We do not want to re-victimize someone by hurting them again with our behavior.

Second, being in a hurry when you ask if they need anything is not effective. Dr. Alan Wolfelt, author and founder of the Center for Loss and Life's Transitions, reminds us that "there is no reward for speed" when helping others.[20] I previously had a boss who was a grief counselor, and I would repeatedly listen to him begin conversations by saying, "I only have a minute but wanted to know how you are doing." He often wondered why people would not be open to sharing with him. I compare it to the hostess clearing the table while guests are still eating. The messages are clear: be quick. The healing power of presence is real. We cannot take someone's pain away but being present is to bear witness to the pain and suffering. The bereaved must move toward the pain to ultimately heal, so be courageous to stand alongside them.

---

[20] D. Alan Wolfelt, *Companioning the Bereaved: A Soulful Guide for Counselors and Caregivers* (Fort Collins, CO: Companion, 2006), p.60.

Remember you are not responsible for fixing or healing them. There is no technique or formula that you can follow but to honor and respect the grieving process. Wolfelt states, "Bearing witness to the struggles of someone experiencing the darkness of grief—having empathy—is the deepest form of emotional and spiritual interaction you can have with another human being."[21]

Many times, we want to be doing or saying something, as we think it is more helpful than inaction. When I worked as a counselor for a funeral home, I often was requested to be with families during the initial visits to the funeral home. During one family's tragedy, I had plans to go on vacation and had a back-up counselor that was well-known in the community ready to step in for me. She listened to my request and then asked me, "Where is the list?" I responded quizzically by repeating her question, "The list?" She then replied, "Yes, the list of what I should say to them." At that moment, I knew she did not understand the power of presence. I rearranged my plans, and I was with the family when they arrived to see their precious young daughter's body. I told them if they wanted to talk, I would listen. But if not, I would just be available. I did not say or do anything in those ninety minutes they were there. I listened. I stood next to them, and that was all.

As they left, they said to the funeral director, "Thanks so much for having the counselor here; it was helpful." He asked me what I did to help them. I was present. I was brave. I understood that there was no list, nothing I could say at that moment to make anything better. You don't need a list either nor certain qualifications to be there for your friend. Just be willing to sit in silence and rest on the power of presence.

---

[21] Wolfelt, *Companioning the Bereaved*, p.60.

 **QUICK TIPS**

- You are not alone; the Holy Spirit is there, too. Seek support. Pray.
- Keep a journal. A private space to write your feelings about the pain you are witnessing.
- Be realistic. Keep perspective. Jesus didn't heal everyone; why do we think we need to?
- Recognize limitations. If it becomes too much, don't just walk away. Refer them to additional support. Be honest and clear about what you can provide.
- Forgive yourself for not being able to do all you would like to do for your friends/loved ones.
- You will be touched. Witnessing pain and being present to mourning will change you. A deeper meaning to what is important is the greatest lesson death/grief teaches, and that every moment should be lived to the fullest.
- Be comfortable with silence: just being there, silent, is still being supportive and ready to listen. Give the bereaved person the airspace if they feel like talking.

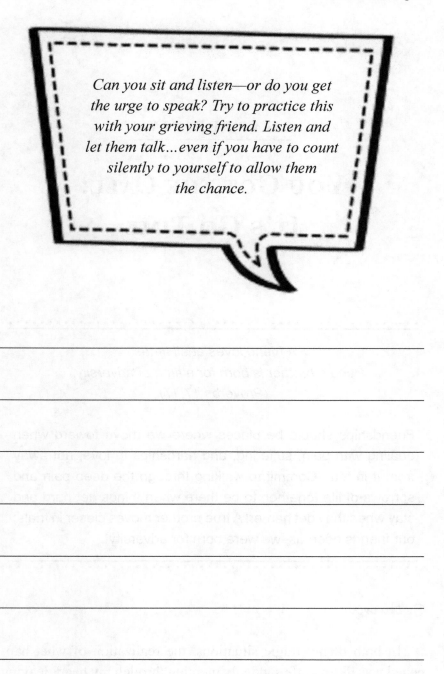

Can you sit and listen—or do you get the urge to speak? Try to practice this with your grieving friend. Listen and let them talk...even if you have to count silently to yourself to allow them the chance.

_____

_____

_____

_____

_____

_____

CHAPTER FIVE

You Got the Call: It's Go Time

....

A friend loves at all times,
and a brother is born for a time of adversity.
(Proverbs 17:17)

Friendships should be places where we move toward when dealing with pain, suffering, and hardships in love, not away from it in fear. Commit to walking through the deep pain and sorrows of life together, to be there when things get hard and stay when they get harder! A true brother moves closer in trials; our friends need us—we were born for adversity!

....

Bethany

In both of my tragic situations, the realization of what happened was like a knife suddenly piercing through my heart, leaving me stunned and short of breath. Neither situation could have been anticipated; I was in shock and panic mode. Many people quickly surrounded me, but I alone had to make big decisions—and fast. It was helpful to allow others to handle the less critical decisions and tasks so I could focus on what I needed to do. The normal everyday tasks from feeding the dog to paying a bill to not letting the wet laundry sit in the washer for days, everything had to be done, even though they weren't my top priorities. There was so much to be done right away—too much for one person to handle without help. Mary Beth Chapman, the author of *Choosing to See,* recalls the multitude of decisions and the friends that were there for them after the death of their daughter. Friends were available to "help us think." They were also there to "offer their support and love, to be sad and broken with us."[22]

Since you're here to help your grieving friend, there are plenty of ways to meet the immediate needs if you are able. I'm going to share the most critical areas in which you can offer support immediately following a loss, meaning in the days and weeks following. In other situations where the loss is not sudden, but rather expected, there still may be immediate needs that you can help with, although some plans and preparations may have already been made or started.

Immediate Needs: Help Wanted

In her book, *Choosing to See*, Mary Beth Chapman talks about her journey before and after the sudden death of her child. She was at the hospital, just having said a final goodbye to her young daughter. Friends had come to the hospital to comfort the family, and she intended to greet them. Someone had been sent back to the house to get clean clothes for her, as hers had blood on them, and

[22] Mary Beth Chapman, *Choosing to See* (Grand Rapids: Revell, 2010), p.154.

she knew that would be a scary sight to see. Mary Beth explained to her friends that she didn't want to wait for her clothes to be brought to her; she wanted to go now to the people who had gathered at the hospital to support them. She asked her close friends if they could give her their clothes. As good friends would do, without hesitation, in the hospital bathroom they stripped off their own clothes—one handed her a shirt and bra and another their pants. Mary Beth recalled the moment being "almost funny."

She asked her friends to wait there so when the person returned from her house with other clothes, they could come out of the bathroom.[23] If you are one of the close friends of the grieving person, do whatever it takes to help them in their hour of need. Literally, you can give your friend the shirt off your back if she needs it.

Whether or not you are the best person for these immediate needs depends on your relationship with the newly grieving person and who it was that died. You can offer and if the grieving person already has this covered, then kindly step back. There are and will be plenty of opportunities for people to help. Some of these immediate roles are as follows:

Communicator: Allow the grieving person to decide which people they want to tell personally of the news. Beyond that, if you have a gentle and respectful way of expressing news, you can offer to communicate the information with the grieving person's explicit permission. If you're not sure what to say, ask God to give you the words and He will. I would also recommend asking the grieving person if they are comfortable with what you intend to say to others. For example, "If you'd like me to let our closest neighbors know, I'd be willing to do that." If the grieving person says yes, let them know who you intend to tell, what you are going to say, and make sure they approve of your words. An example would be, "If

---

you approve, I will tell these five neighbors and just let them know he died, that you are safe, and to keep you in their thoughts." If the neighbors want to reach out, or help in a specific way, let them know you will pass the offer along and you will get back to them. If the neighbors want to write down how they are willing to help in a card that would be even better for helping to keep track of offers.

You can discuss if the person wants anything to be put on social media or not. For some grieving people, they want to get the news out as quickly as possible. For others, they may prefer privacy, even just for a few days. If the grieving person requests or accepts your offer to post on social media on their behalf, remember to focus on the reason for the post: is it to get information out so people are aware, is it to request prayer and/or help, or some other reason? As we know, once news is "out there," we cannot take it back. Make sure it is respectful and doesn't invite more hassle for the newly grieving person. Please be careful not to tell more details than are necessary—you might not know the whole story. Speaking from experience, it's disappointing and causes more stress when others self-proclaim the role of communicator and spread the word to more people than truly "need to know" and give (erroneous) details without checking with the grieving person first. Respect their wishes, especially when there are tricky circumstances or details associated with the death or loss. I have a wise friend who once explained that in cases of the desire to spread information, even though it may affect you, it may not be your story to tell.

Service/will coordinator: Some people have planned their funeral, the arrangements, and maybe even paid for their funeral in advance. I am guessing this is the minority, especially for younger people. When a sudden death happens, there are critical decisions to be made in a relatively short amount of time. If you are a person close to the griever, you may play a role in helping with these critical decisions. The first question to ask is, "Did they have a will?"

which will specify any requests or directives regarding arrangements. Secondly, do they know where the will is and can you help find it? It might be in a bank security box, a safe, or a filing cabinet. If you are a trusted close friend or family member, you can also offer to read and interpret the will but wait for the griever's permission to do so. If the services are not already planned, you could offer to call funeral homes and get ideas about the process and options. If the grieving person has a church home, you can offer to contact them and see what they require for a service–gather the information and provide it. If the grieving person does not have a church home, the funeral home is the best place to start.

Hydration Helper: A great idea shared by my own co-author is that of helping bereaved people and their visiting guests to stay hydrated. As soon as she can after the loss, Gwen drops off an insulated cooler (think even the Styrofoam disposable cooler with lid), fills it with ice and beverages like water, soda, and sports drinks and sets it on their porch. She tells or texts the grieving person that if the cooler needs a refill to just text her and she will do so as many times or for as long as is needed. When you are able, you can drive by and check on the cooler and replenish it as needed. Depending on how well you know the family you can write a bible verse on the side or write an encouraging note, even, "Stay hydrated." Why is this such an important thing? A lot of talking, a lot of crying, a lot of emotions can be cause for dehydration. Sleep and water are critical. Grieving people often have many visitors and while they shouldn't expect to be fed, per se, it is nice to have drinks available. If the cooler is on the porch, you aren't interrupting the grieving person or burdening them. When Gwen told me that she does this I was grateful for her heart and thoughtful service to grieving people. Whether you know the family well or not, this is a relatively easy way to be of great help. I'm thinking right now especially of those helpers that are easing their way into grief support, still somewhat afraid of awkward confrontations…this is a great place to start! Maybe you are shy about sharing aloud bible verses… write it on the cooler you deliver! It's never too late to start sharing hope with steps like these.

Cleaner: While it is natural for those gathering around the grieving person to help around the house, start laundry, and tidy up, please do not wash the deceased person's laundry right away. It may sound strange, but when someone experiences a death, they want evidence of their person: their shoes, their clothes, their handwriting. Don't get rid of any of it right away. My mom, who had rushed to my house to help, was taking care of what she could. I noticed that she was about to wash the towels, including the one Kevin had used just that morning. I quickly stopped her and asked her not to wash it as I was afraid it would "erase" the smell of Kevin. The towel did, of course, get washed at some point but when I felt ready to do so. My helpful mom continued doing chores around the house but was careful about touching items that belonged to Kevin.

It's best to leave the deceased's belongings where they are until the grieving person wants something done with them. You could help by offering to wash other things, do the dishes, clean the bathrooms, or do other household chores. Those tasks are helpful when it is likely that many visitors will be coming and going in the next few days. Housework is the last item on the priority list for the grieving person, yet, they don't want to have to worry about the state of their house. Mowing the lawn, raking leaves, and snow-shoveling are all super helpful and don't necessarily require permission from the grieving person. When I saw a neighbor mowing my lawn the day after my husband died, I just smiled and sighed in gratefulness. It may not have been a big deal for him, but it was for me.

Fundraiser: If it is suspected that finances are going to be a big need for the grieving person, please don't jump on GoFundMe without weighing out some options. First, the bereaved should give permission to do such a campaign, including the means/method of collecting and the goal amount. If approved, consider the available choices. GoFundMe is a popular option because it's user-friendly. However, while it is free to set up a campaign, the company they use to process the payment keeps a small percentage of the funds donated. This is also true for GiveSendGo.com. Other options are contacting a local bank and asking if they would be willing to be the collector of funds and deposit them into an account in the name of the grieving person, especially easy if the person is an existing customer. If you explain the situation, most banks are willing to help. There are electronic transfers, such as PayPal, Zelle, and Venmo, to name a few where the money is transferred directly to that person's account.

If the money is to benefit children, ask the grieving person if they have existing savings or education accounts already set up where money could be directed. If you collect cash or electronic funds to be given to the grieving person, make sure to clearly document the amount, from whom (if known), and the date you gave it to the recipient. Money certainly is helpful; just be sure you've helped the grieving person explore options before diving into the most common donation site you think of without reading the fine print.

Screener: You might find yourself in a position of being able to screen callers and visitors. Most likely, you are staying with the grieving person (or currently live there). Start notebooks with the following titles:

Notebook #1: Messages/Visitors

- Anytime someone calls, do not automatically hand the phone to the grieving person. Ask who is calling and let the caller know you will check to see if they are available. Let your friend decide if they want to talk to that person at that moment. If not, write down who it was, the date and time, their message and call back number. Assure the caller you will deliver the message. The grieving person might like to know everyone who called, even if they weren't able to take the call, or they weren't available. Let them call people back when they are ready.

- If anyone stops by to visit, the same may apply as with a phone call. The grieving person can decide if they want to come out and talk to the visitor or not or have them come inside. If you are the person who is "screening" visitors and calls, kindly let the visitor know that you will let the griever know they stopped by. You can offer to take their phone numbers and write down a message from them.

- If anyone provides food, supplies, or gifts, record this in the notebook for your friend's information. The grieving person should not feel obligated to send a thank-you card on top of everything else going on, but they will want to know at some point, if they don't realize it now, who provided help to them.

Notebook #2: Immediate

These are calls and tasks that should be done within a few days, not necessarily meaning that you should be the one to do them. These are helpful to the grieving person, but it is up to them if they will do them or delegate them to trusted others to do. I give credit for this idea to my brother. After my tragedies, my brother dropped everything and drove hours to help me. Among other helpful things, he bought me folders and notebooks. He took the initiative to label and prioritize what needed to be done and made calls for me when I couldn't think and didn't want to talk to anyone. Items for the immediate notebook include:

- Notifying employers of the loss and what needs to be done immediately, if anything.
- Funeral home calls/appointments.
- Locating the will if one exists.
- Church calls, if applicable—notify the person's home church of the loss, and gather notes for what options are available through the church (luncheons, cost, dates).
- List of relatives the grieving person wants to be notified and who is to notify them. Maybe it's the communicator above; maybe it's another person. Make sure the grieving person decides what information they want given out. There is no reason the grieving person should have to call everyone, but it is up to their preference and family dynamic. Be clear in the instructions to these people about what information and means are appropriate to share. For example, "Beth prefers this information is not put out on social media at this time, and she appreciates you understanding that."
- The grieving person's medical doctor, if they are having trouble sleeping or with anxiety related to the loss. The doctor may recommend prescribing a short-term medication to get them through the first week. Sleep is very important, so if the grieving person and their doctor agree it is a good idea, respect that.
- The grieving person's counselor, if applicable. If they do not have a counselor currently, this can likely wait a few weeks or more for the grieving person to get through the initial demands of the loss.

- School/day-care. If a child is affected, it is a good idea to notify their school/day care not only so they are aware they might not be there for some time, but so there is a plan in place for their return. What is the plan if they are struggling, need to talk to a counselor or need to sit out of certain activities, given the circumstances?

Notebook #3: Non-Urgent

These are calls and tasks that are necessary but not critical within the first week, typically. Listing them in a notebook will help sort out what needs to be done.

- Calling mortgage companies, credit card companies, banks, and other billers and letting them know there is a current personal hardship, and you're wondering if you can get a month's grace period (if there is uncertainty with finances).
- Calling life insurance companies.
- Ordering death certificates, which is guided by the funeral home. I suggest ordering multiple; it costs less than ordering more down the road. They will be needed occasionally for proof.
- Making an appointment at the Social Security office.
- Consider contacting a lawyer/estate attorney to interpret the will and process, if necessary. Beware of contacts originating from wrongful death attorneys who seek out people to represent. Sadly, there are situations in which grieving people can be taken advantage of. However, there are reputable attorneys who offer a free consultation when requested. This is an area where friends and family might be able to help make recommendations.
- Calling a financial planner that offers a free consultation to review the grieving person's financial situation. This

usually comes two to three months post-loss after the dust somewhat settles.

- Utility, cable, cell phone, mortgage, and other companies to remove the deceased person from the account. In some cases, it doesn't really matter. Many years post-loss, my husband is still on my property taxes and electric bill, but I am an authorized account holder. In other cases, the grieving person needs to make changes to the account. This can be a huge hassle, but necessary.

- Before canceling the cell phone of the deceased person, be sure to have their voicemail greeting and/or messages preserved if you can. I used a company I found on the internet that recorded my husband's voicemail greeting and emailed it to me so I can always listen to his four-second greeting. It was worth the thirty or so dollars it cost.

- If applicable, make an appointment at the Secretary of State's office for updating a driver's license and/or transferring ownership of an automobile/watercraft into a different name.

- Review the cable or internet bill, if applicable. Are there changes you can make that may reduce the bill? If the deceased person loved sports but the grieving person never watched sports, it might be worth seeing if there is a less expensive package without that item.

- Contact the doctor of the deceased person. If interested, you can order their medical file for your records. This isn't something all grieving people would do, but if so, it's best to do it within six months, as the doctor's office may no longer keep the file on site, and it would be harder to obtain it down the road. Why would the grieving person want this? You just never know. There could be eventual questions from descendants of the deceased person that want to know specifics about their medical history.

Though it is natural for a grieving person to quickly panic about finances if there is an unexpected loss, it is recommended to try and avoid making any major decisions for the first year, if possible. This includes selling the house or other major property. What you can do, as a supportive person helping the grieving person, is listen and offer resources should the topic arise about selling/moving/donating items, but also encourage them to not rush into these decisions if they don't have to. You can help explore the options, knowing it is their ultimate decision. Chances are, the decision to sell, donate, or move items is not an easy one, and it would not be supportive to make them feel guilty or question their decision.

Organizer: One thing you can offer if the grieving person indicates they want/need to sell or donate items, despite it being a fresh loss, is to manage that process. You can help research the value, take pictures of the items, and help the grieving person find options for the sale or donation. Again, there is usually no rush to sell personal belongings, like clothes, shoes, and hobby-related items or tools. Big-ticket items, especially if not owned outright, may have a more urgent timeline. I would refrain from pressuring the grieving person to sell or donate any item without at least some passing of time and careful thought. For most personal items, there should be no rush because once items are gone, they are gone. There may be people in the family interested in buying them or having them, or the items may be able to be saved for children when they grow up.

I had a very unfortunate situation after my second tragedy. I had a "friend" quickly offer to take a carload of specialized items (since I had inherited them) and sell them for me. I was grateful because I had no knowledge of the value of these items, trusted my friend, and was concerned about finances. The offer included logging items on a spreadsheet to be shared with me. Instead, the person did not communicate well, I never had a record of the items despite my requests, and I didn't receive money for all the items.

At one point, I respectfully requested they return the unsold items, that I was grateful for the work they had done to try and sell them but didn't want this to be a burden for them. They refused to return the unsold items until I ultimately had to mention small claims court as a resolution option. They ended up returning one or two items, finally, after many of my voicemails (and a lot of tears and frustration). To add salt to the wound, they calculated the value of an item less their labor cost to work on my vehicle's brakes (that they had completed two years prior as a favor to me!) This situation ruined our friendship.

If the grieving person trusts you to help sell or donate belongings, take pictures of the items first and log each one in a document or email. In this document, also include the price sold and if possible, where/who the item went to. If the grieving person trusts you, don't be a jerk. Follow through and be honest. If it gets to be too burdensome or doesn't work out the way you hoped, be clear and return the items or help find another solution.

Gwen

By the time we say it's "go" time for a wedding, usually months or even years of planning and preparation have occurred. When it is "go" time for a birth, books have been read, classes taken, and breathing has been practiced. Often a birth plan has been completed and a bag has been packed, unless you didn't know you were pregnant; in that case, you can be featured on the show about surprise births. On the contrary, in a death situation, especially a sudden death, there has been very little, if any, preparation. Most mourners come to the job of grieving feeling inadequate and certainly not ever ready.

In author Jon Acuff's book, *Soundtracks*, he features wise words from Zig Ziglar, the forefather of motivational thought in America. Zig said, "It's not what happens to you that determines how far you will go in life; it is how you handle what happens to you." He taught the difference between reacting (which is negative) and responding (which is positive), sharing that the important difference is, "You plan in advance how you are going to respond."[24] Here lies the key to being a supporter: prepare in advance. You are ahead of the game if you are reading this book either way, before or just after you are called to duty.

We encourage you to find your role and do that well, rather than the temptation to do all things and do them poorly. Maybe your part is finding others to fill the needed roles. This can be such a gift to the bereaved person who knows they have many needs, yet does not have the mental capacity, nor the energy, to find someone to fill them.

This can also be the time when hurt, due to unfulfilled expectations, can happen. When working with the bereaved, I ask them to step back and see if their expectations of others are realistic. Maybe we are asking our doer to be a listener (or vice versa), or we are asking our spiritual care person to help with the phone bill. You too can step back and look at what is expected of you: is it a perceived expectation or real? I think that is an important clarification for you. Are you putting pressure or expectations on yourself based on your role or relationship with the bereaved? If you are finding yourself helping in a role that really isn't you, please say so. It is healthy and okay for the helper to have boundaries. It is not selfish or uncaring if you state your role, meaning, "This is how I can help you" and/or "This is not something I can do right now." The major factor here is communicating this during the stressful and overwhelming first days. So, my guidance would be to take the time and not only grieve, too, but look at where you and your strengths fit into their needs.

---

[24] Jon Acuff, *Soundtracks* (Grand Rapids: Baker Books, 2021), p. 141.

Different Types of Helpers

There are many types of helpers, some not as helpful as others.

Not as Helpful

Over-identifiers: They tend to jump in and save the day. They make the point that they are "in charge and know exactly what is needed," and everyone gets the message loud and clear. Usually, this results in others backing off, and the grieving person is left with a dominant helper trying to run their life and, many times, making problems. It becomes more about them and their desire to run the show rather than what the family needs. I have experienced this in my own personal life. In addition to my professional experience and not being afraid to address hard things, I knew I could be of help, yet I was bullied by an over-identifier and walked away. I have struggled with my decision to back off and have had to apologize for my behavior. My advice is to gently stand firm because the over-helper is often very persistent. But, you don't want to look back with regret and know that if you had remained consistent in the help you could provide, the griever would have benefited.

Abandoners: These helpers are quick to say, "Just call if you need me," yet never show up or follow through. It is mainly all talk, no action. Bereaved people often say they hear many people express concern through the quick "How are you?" conversations at the mailbox or the bathroom at church, yet when it comes to really being there, only a few are left for those jobs. Sympathy is good, too. A simple "I am so sorry" in a card or spoken word is nice, but not necessarily helpful. The motto at the school of social work I attended was, "It is nice to be nice, but it is more helpful to be helpful."

Most Helpful

Boundary-setters: This type of helper sets boundaries and keeps their promises or will let you know if they cannot. They offer tangible things they can and will do. Some examples:

> "I can make your kids lunch for the next two weeks, so you don't have to think about that."

> "I will drop off pizza every Friday night this month."

> "I am going to the store. What can I pick up for you?"

Teachable helpers: One who has a teachable spirit says,

> "Teach me what this is like for you."

> "Would it be helpful if_____?" (Fill in the blank—and then let the bereaved person decide whether it is, so we are not assuming what is helpful.)

When helping bereaved people to engage or expand their support network, discuss the roles that are needed and identify people who can fill those roles. Many times, adult children are expected to fill all the roles when their parent or parents have died, and that is not realistic or the best use of people.

For example, my brother is a "doer," responding in an awesome way when my recently widowed mother asks him for help. He pays her bills, fixes things around the house, and assists in making decisions. My mother, however, has expressed frustration at his lack of phone calls and no-agenda visits. I interceded and explained that those are not his skill set or comfort zone. Therefore, it is not a realistic expectation for my mom to have that my brother will engage

79

in much small talk or proactively check in. No one is "wrong" in this example, but it takes communication and a level of understanding of where each person is at.

Another helpful tip is to divide the jobs up so that we aren't assuming someone else is already taking care of certain tasks. Ideally, we try to stay within each person's desired area of help. If a need arises that no one wants to meet, talk about it and take turns completing it. It is a simple "Who wants to _____?" No matter the size of the family or support network, it is good to spread out the workload and not expect too much from a few.

The last thought in these early days of grief is to remind yourself that the bereaved person is in a literal fog. They may not be remembering anything … This is where they need direction. Very few times in life do adults need someone else to push or pull them, but this may be one. Also, they are adjusting and reacting to most likely the single most devastating thing that has happened to them. They may be experiencing sleepless, long nights and doing the exhausting work that grief requires. I say this to remind you that as you read and learn about your role, be patient and gentle with your friend in their new role as a griever too.

What kind of helper do you want to be?

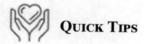 **QUICK TIPS**

- Helpers very clearly state what they can do and what they cannot do.
- Be organized and document what you've done, whether it's maintaining paperwork or helping with the sale or donation of goods. This will help your friend know what was done and who did it.
- Setting boundaries is always good and helpful.
- Follow through on what you said you would do.
- If you cannot complete your tasks, do not just walk away, but explain that you cannot continue to help right now and/ or find someone who can complete the task.

You Got the Call: It's Go Time

Can you identify with these types of helpers? Do you know an over-identifier? Have you ever felt abandoned when you needed help?

_____

_____

_____

_____

_____

_____

CHAPTER SIX

GROCERY STORE GRIEF AND THINKING OUTSIDE THE PASTA POT

Then he lay down under the bush and fell asleep. All at once an angel touched him and said, "Get up and eat." He looked around, and there by his head was some bread baked over hot coals, and a jar of water. He ate and drank and then lay down again. The angel of the LORD came back a second time and touched him and said, "Get up and eat, for the journey is too much for you." (1 Kings 19:5–7)

God's servant Elijah was alone, exhausted, frightened, and trying to outrun trouble. Yet in these verses, we see how God provides for his needs, even the physical ones. He knows that many of life's difficult journeys require food, water, and rest. He knows we need our strength and is the supplier, many times through willing servants, to meet our needs.

Bethany

Typically, when a death happens, family and friends rush to the side of the grieving person. Guests are at their house, and food is often provided by others. Sometimes there is enough food and meals for weeks following the death. Eventually though, the grieving person must make a trip to the grocery store to replenish their pantry. Carefully read this reality: the grocery store can be one of the most traumatic errands following the death of a person who lived with you. It's hard to understand unless you've experienced it.

Crying over bananas

A peek into my first grocery store visit after my husband died:

I grabbed a cart and headed toward the first fruit stand I saw: bananas. Great, yes, I decided to grab a bunch. Kevin had just been saying the other day bananas sounded good... Oh (sigh), Kevin. Kev-in ... it doesn't matter what he said sounded good. It will never matter again what he said he wanted, what he likes to eat. Kevin will never eat another banana. He died three weeks ago. I had never, nor since, sobbed over a bunch of bananas.

Grieving people who finally go out and grocery shop are painfully reminded that they don't need to shop for the people in their lives who have died. What they liked, what they requested, it doesn't matter. A routine task like this can bring about anxiety, stress, waves of sadness, and genuine heartache for your grieving friend. It might not always be so, but right now it does. Grieving people in a grocery store often look at other shoppers with a bit of jealousy and think, *their life appears normal while mine is falling apart.* The people grumbling about their Starbucks coffee order being wrong have no idea that your life circumstances are wrong.

If you see someone crying at the banana stand, don't give them a judgmental look. They might be grieving.

To help ease the stress of this "grocery store grief," ask your friend if they'd like company to go grocery shopping, or if you can shop for them. With the abundance of shopping services like Shipt and Instacart, arranging grocery delivery is another option. Eventually, the grieving person will need to face the grocery store, or any other form of shopping, but easing them into this task is a helpful offer. Consider letting them know you're already at the store and asking them what you can pick up for them. This helps with any burden they might feel about asking for help in this area.

Grieving People Need to Eat Too

Food is often the first thing people decide they must offer: "I'll make food. Yes. That is what they need." I would agree it is helpful when people provide meals. In some cases, the cost of food can be an issue with a reduced income and higher expenses. Universally, the difficulty is in the tasks themselves (buying, cooking, eating) and the decreased number of people now they now need to feed. Besides that, grieving people are often in physical pain, due to emotional stress and have little to no appetite. Cooking for fewer people often changes the type of food the grieving person makes and they, in turn, may miss meals they used to enjoy. There are immediate meal needs and there are long-term meal needs. Months later, when much of the support fades away and the grieving person is expected to get back to their routine, often having to return to work, meals can be a tangible blessing.

Consider the Long Haul

If you are the type of person prone to procrastination, I'm here to tell you: you are a winner! While other helpers provided food at the onset of your friend's grief, your "late to the party" response in providing a meal is fine and even desired. My friend, and grieving mother Sharisse suggested offering meals months later. She explained that initially, after the death of her young son, she had a lot of family around her, and meals were nice to have for everyone. [25] Eventually, she returned to work and was too tired at the end of the day from continual grief and ongoing life. She felt overwhelmed. Meals spread out over a longer period are part of a helpful solution for this. Showing the grieving person that you haven't forgotten them and want to bless them is a good idea. It is never too late to provide help in this area.

My friend, Laura, adds that her sister-in-law provided their family a meal once a week for eight months while her son received treatment for cancer. The helper didn't just offer a meal and check it off her list— "provided a meal—check!" She continued providing because she knew this was a long process. Some weeks, the family would put the meal in the freezer but some weeks, it was consumed that night. There were so many variations in their schedule, it was nice to count on one meal from someone else. If you can make a double batch of a meal or have leftovers, call up your grieving friend and ask if you can bring it over for them even months into their journey.

---

[25] Personal Communication with author, November 9, 2023, Used with permission.

Lasagna: The Death Food

Before you scoff at lasagna being called "the death food," hear me out. It seems to be the go-to meal to make for those who are mourning or going through a tough time. I get it; lasagna is beneficial for many reasons. It serves a big family; it freezes; it reheats well; there are different varieties; most people like it. Except when they are given five different pans of it. Then it becomes "the death food," as called by bereaved mom Tonya who received many versions of the Italian classic.

After Tonya's young daughter died, she still had two other children, a husband, an exchange student, and other family to provide for. Please don't think she wasn't grateful for the multiple lasagnas—she was. But when someone is dealing with grief, shock, changes in every aspect of her life, so much uncertainty, and a not-so-great appetite anyway, having to force herself to eat the same food for weeks is not ideal. Upon meeting others at grief support groups, conversation would lead into the ways people have been helpful. For the first time in weeks, Tonya laughed out loud at a lasagna conversation with other grieving people who agreed they couldn't bear to look at another pan of the commonly gifted dish. It might have been her first actual LOL, in fact, after her loss.

Lasagna disclaimer: for those that have and continue to make lasagna for grieving families, I am not discouraging you from doing so. If that is your gift, keep giving it. Just know it is not the only option of a dish to make, and it might be good to ask the grieving person if they've already received a few lasagnas before offering yours. You could consider asking the grieving person if they have any requests for meals they would like you to make.

Let's Taco-About: Alternative Meal Ideas, Including Frozen

Pasta does tend to be easy, filling, and enjoyed by most. But if you are willing to be a little creative, it might break the monotony of a grieving person's meal deliveries. What about a taco bar? Include cooked taco meat (easy to re-heat and can be frozen), sour cream/ Greek yogurt, bagged lettuce, tortilla chips, salsa, and cheese. This is easy for the giver and easy for the receiver. I've made many different taco/enchilada/burrito meals that also freeze well—there are plenty of options on the internet.

Giving a freezer meal to a grieving family is a great idea, too. Make sure to let them know it will take overnight to thaw in the refrigerator so they can plan accordingly. Make sure the meal is clearly labeled (what it is, when it was made, ingredients and reheating/baking/cooking instructions). Use a permanent marker to write on the container. You can buy disposable containers & lids that are freezer and oven-safe. Don't request or expect to get your container back and make that clear to the person when it is delivered. I've often made multiple batches of meals that I could freeze portions of to have ready for delivery to someone who needs it. Meals that a family can just thaw in the refrigerator overnight and put in the oven the next day are huge blessings. Making freezer meals is also a fun activity for a small group of friends, where they can make some for themselves and some to give away.

Meal-Organizing Sites

Thank goodness there are several great options for meal planning for a grieving person. There are websites like Takethemameal. com, mealtrain.com, giveinkind.com, and signupgenius.com, where you can include many people to sign up for a meal delivery day. Don't assume someone is already orchestrating meals. Ask. If no one has stepped forward, be the someone. The person organizing it does not have to be one of the grieving person's closest friends but does need to have a basic conversation about their food preferences and who should be invited to participate. It could be offered on a Facebook page, mentioned in a church bulletin, emailed, or spread word of mouth. Participants might include members of the family, church, co-workers, friends, and neighbors, among others. The food preferences can be stated on the website so it can specify any allergies and foods to avoid, tailoring it to their liking. Participants then sign up easily and enter what they plan to make. Some of these websites have suggested meal ideas and recipes and even ordering/delivering of food. This makes the process easy for the grieving person, as they can see what is on the meal for the day and who will be bringing it. Changes can be made instantly if it turns out they don't need a meal on a particular day.

The actual meal delivery process can be decided by the coordinator and recipient. Some recipients are open to receiving the meal in person, but some don't feel comfortable with this. They might not be in the mood to chit-chat; they might be experiencing a wave of grief and don't want to make the meal provider uncomfortable. However, some meal recipients welcome the company and want conversation for a change. Realize that these decisions might be last-minute, depending on the grieving person's emotions at that time. Don't be offended. Cater to their needs and requests. It is about them, not you. Some meal recipients place a large cooler outside of their door for the deliverer to place the meal in, which allows the recipient to retrieve it on their own.

One family, whose daughter passed away, was given a refrigerator/freezer that was placed in a pole barn. Meal delivery instructions were to not drive up to the family's house, but rather take the side driveway to the pole barn and put the dish inside the refrigerator. This gave the family privacy and prevented them from having to face people and repeat the story or current emotional state every time a generous donor delivered a meal.

Please don't be offended if the grieving person wants meal delivery this way. Remember, it is not about you getting credit for cooking the meal or telling others you spoke with the grieving person. It is about serving someone who is mourning and doing what is best for them.

One friend who signed up to bring me a meal texted me at night, saying, "I'm picking up Applebee's for you tomorrow if that's okay–let me know what you'd like." This was perfect. I hadn't been out to eat in months, and to be able to "order" something felt like a real treat. What a great idea.

Another friend who signs up to bring meals often uses a chain restaurant take-out as her go-to meal delivery. They are "homemade"-type meals that still make it possible for this busy mother of three to be able to provide a meal.

Gift cards to restaurants are also valuable. There are days when the hurting person doesn't want to make dinner. They may not have the groceries stocked to be able to make it happen or the energy to do so. Eating out, whether dining in or take-out, is a treat for a lot of people, and having gift cards on hand enables the grieving person to treat themselves without financial burden or guilt. However, if you've signed up to bring an actual meal that can be eaten that day, don't just deliver a gift card. That entails more than the grieving person may be able to do that day if they were counting on a meal ready to eat.

Invite Them Out

An alternative to bringing a meal is to invite them to meet you at a restaurant, stating it is your treat. It can be hard for grieving people to go out to a restaurant where they might dine alone or hear laughter when they feel like crying. Depending on the situation and the grieving person's comfort level, offer to drive them to and from the restaurant or meet them there. Be sure to mention that you are willing to leave the restaurant if they feel uncomfortable. Some grieving people may want to drive themselves in case they want to be able to determine when they can leave. Consider letting them choose the restaurant, the table location (they might want to sit away from tables with couples or families for example) and let them lead the conversation. They might want to talk about the loss, or they might want to talk about anything but their loss. Be flexible and place no expectations other than showing them love and a nice meal.

Meal Size: Smaller Is Sometimes Better

Portion control is another sticky issue to keep in mind. When my husband died, I received meals that were wonderful, and wonderfully large. Looking back, I guess I should have tried to freeze some of it before baking it, because I ended up with a lot of leftovers. If the grieving person still has family coming around, a larger portion is a benefit. But, if one young widow and her toddler son receive a 9x13 pan of baked pasta, much of it will go to waste. I recommend making two smaller portions so that one portion can be frozen if needed. Loaf pans or 8x8 pans often are a good portion size for a very small family (one adult and one to two young kids). Some people don't mind leftovers, but one can only take so many days of the same food. Having extra food can remind the grieving person that their loved one isn't there to help eat it. I hated it when I had about two portions left, as it reminded me that Kevin, my husband, would have eaten one portion and taken the other for lunch the next day. It's amazing the thoughts about food that go through a grieving person's mind. Because they are constantly reminded of their loss, even food brings back painful memories and sadness.

You can't necessarily calculate how much the grieving person will need and try to prevent them from being sad about their loved one not being able to eat a meal. But, it is just a reminder that grief is heavy and complicated. You are being a huge blessing to them by providing a meal, but just know that it could trigger sadness during the appreciation of the meal. Don't be scared to accidentally make the deceased person's favorite meal; you can't always know these details. If tears fall when the recipient receives the meal, don't be offended or act awkward. Just tell them you care about them, and you hope they can enjoy the meal.

Spur-of-the-moment meals or your own leftovers/excess meals can also be great options. Let's say you cook a large meal for your family and have way too much left over. Instead of letting any go to waste, call up or text the widow down the street or newly divorced dad and ask if they would like a plate or two of food. It doesn't have to be fancy, and they have the right to say, "No thanks" (and don't be offended) if it is because of taste or allergies. I quite often send my son across the street with our dinner extras to give to the older widowed neighbor. I know there is no way he is making a whole meatloaf for himself.

Why Not Breakfast?

One alternative idea is to consider making meals other than dinner. Why not provide breakfast? The sausage/egg/cheese casserole can be made the night before, put in the fridge, and baked when they are ready for it. What about a dish of oatmeal with different toppings? If you are close to the grieving person, you could ask if you could come over and set up a waffle bar. Bring a variety of waffle toppings, your pre-made waffle mix, your waffle iron, paper plates, and plastic forks. If the grieving person insists you can use their tableware, that is fine, but don't assume that is ok. A sink of messy dishes might overwhelm the grieving person, so plan to wash dishes before you leave. For those who don't love to cook, pick up a box of donuts and cider, a bag of bagels and cream cheese, a tray of cut-up fruit, or some muffins and juice.

For some grieving people, they need a specific reason to get up and go in the morning. Knowing they have a breakfast delivery coming, or breakfast food that needs to be eaten, may be the good motivation they need. Boxes of cereal and milk can also be well-received because going to the grocery store for basic pantry items can be a daunting chore. Try calling the grieving person and asking them what kind of coffee you can deliver on a specific day.

I was blessed for several years to have a dear friend as my next-door neighbor. Many times, just when I needed it, there was a knock on the door, followed by me opening it to see her, smiling, with a hot cup of coffee just how I liked it. Sometimes she came in and visited when we were both in our jammies. Sometimes it was just a "here you go, love you!" and she'd leave me in awe at how God had blessed me with her. Remember that the little things matter, even a mug of coffee.

Speaking of mugs, I recently heard of a great idea for an easy way to bless your grieving friend. You simply fill a coffee mug with chocolates, hot cocoa mixes, tea or coffee (really the possibilities are endless) and leave it on their porch with a note that says "here is a hug in a mug" just for them.

Snack Time

Don't forget about snacks and desserts, too, instead of big meals. Homemade cookies or a fancy dessert can be a real treat. Even a container of Oreos left on the front step with a note saying you wanted them to know someone was thinking of them is an appreciated gesture. I once had someone "ding dong-ditch" me one late morning, and I found two bags of Ghirardelli chocolates on the doorstep when I answered. It was honestly (and literally) so sweet. It was better that I didn't have to see the "ditcher" because I was not showered and wasn't feeling very social, so it was a great surprise.

One kind friend brought me two cookies from the hospital cafeteria where she worked. The cookies were famous because they were almost as big as a human head! Years later, my son still fondly recalls those cookies.

Grieving People May Have Strange Eating Habits and Weight Fluctuations

Many people have altered their eating habits from what they were used to. This is normal, and they should adjust in time. They may experience weight fluctuations in either direction. It is not your job to comment or try to prevent it. Encouraging them to eat on a regular basis to keep their body functioning is more important. I beg of you … don't comment on their weight loss or gain. While it is okay to say, "You look good," or "You have such a beautiful smile, I'm glad to see it," don't overdo it or force yourself into a compliment. Grieving spouses aren't getting any attention from their partners anymore, and that can be something they really miss, and can result in lower self-esteem. After a while, the grieving person most likely will get back to where they are supposed to be with their weight.

The important exception to this rule would be if you are genuinely concerned about the grieving person's care of themselves. It is worth it to gently mention your concern to them privately (not to your group of mom friends) with a follow-up to their best friend or family member if you see continued symptoms of unhealthy eating behavior.

Be the hands and feet of Jesus by providing food so the grieving person can focus on other areas of their life. Believe me, they have a lot to do, and their heads are spinning. By providing necessary nourishment, you have eased one of their burdens, blessed them, and helped them take care of their health.

Gwen

The food we buy, the cooking we do, and the fellowship around the table may seem like an ordinary thing when life is good, but when changed forever by death, we realize these are the big things.

Nothing says love like food and flowers. This gesture of showing love is valuable. When facing devastating pain, the tasks of daily living become overwhelming. Breathing is about all the bereaved can do at the beginning; hence, the value of all the suggestions in this chapter is extraordinary. Grief and its reactions are very physical, and affecting appetite is very common. As a caring friend or family, we want to *do* something, and cooking is one of the first things that come to mind. Since our culture no longer has symbols of grief (wearing black or adorning mourning jewelry), others do not know what we are going through. Imagine if while crying over the bananas, Bethany could see others who were grieving, and they could bond without saying a word ... knowing they were in the same "club" and instantly normalizing the tears in the produce section. The pressure to look "normal" is often what keeps the bereaved from going out in public, and they begin to withdraw from social contact.

The pain of loss is not something we complete in one fell swoop but rather in bits and pieces, over a period, and when the pain is not so intense. That is why our hurting friends may engage in things we find "weird" or "odd."

An example from a former client of mine conveys this concept. When visiting with a woman who was married for over sixty years, she shared with me that on her first Sunday married to her husband, he explained that he loved Brussels sprouts, and he would like them with every Sunday dinner. Wanting to please her husband, she cooked them every Sunday for their entire marriage but never ate them herself. After her husband died, she asked me if she was ridiculous because she still purchased and cooked them on Sundays. Good question. To the outside world, one that is not in deep pain, this may seem crazy. I assured her that she did not just stop doing loving things for our person so soon after they die; it is an adjustment that takes time.

Six months after his death, when I asked about the Brussels sprouts, she told me that she still buys them, but on Sundays, she looks at them and throws them away. This act is still not odd, and I could see she was adjusting. After fourteen months since his death, she shared that she no longer buys them. She looks at them in the store and thinks of him, but that is all. Keep this in mind if your grieving friend is slowly letting go of traditions—it takes time, and they are not crazy. I would like to take this time to remind you not to ask "Why" questions. When we begin a sentence with why, it puts the receiver on the defensive. Imagine if the client said she buys and cooks Brussels sprouts and no one eats them, and I responded with a "Why would you do that?" I think you get the point. As in many other things in their grief ... it is okay to talk about some of the behaviors that they find themselves doing. They want to share about the "weird" or "odd" things they do, so you can ask. It is okay to do so, it can be therapeutic and better for them than any lasagna!

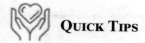 **QUICK TIPS**

- Consider providing breakfast instead of dinner.
- Homemade desserts, specialty cookies/cupcakes.
- Taco bar (cooked meat, shells, cheese, salsa, chips).
- Meals that are good reheated (pastas).
- Set up a meal schedule on a website.
- Consider providing meals for months down the road.
- Ordering food for delivery, Door Dash, Uber Eats, etc.
- Restaurant gift cards, especially those that offer curbside take-out.
- Bringing two to three portions of leftovers from your own meals.
- Invite them out to eat with you, driving them or meeting them at the restaurant (give option).
- Be aware of portions regarding size of family (9x13 dish versus 8x8 dish, or two smaller portions).
- Use disposable containers and cutlery.

What is your favorite comfort food? Which idea(s) in this chapter sound most like what you would/will provide to your friend?

_____

_____

_____

_____

_____

_____

CHAPTER SEVEN

TANGIBLE AND INTANGIBLE GIFTS

I thank my God every time I remember you.
(Philippians 1:3)

Paul wrote to the church in Philippi when he was imprisoned, experiencing pain and troubling circumstances. He allowed the memories of his friends to give him strength and support. The Greek word mimnesko for "remembrance" refers to "mention" or "recollection."[26] Not just the memories, but the mere mention of their names resulted in thanksgiving. Therefore, the gifts that we give in memory of a life that was lived are so treasured.

Bethany

A natural reaction when wanting to help a grieving person is to give them a tangible gift or serve them in some way. Many people decide to send flowers or a plant to the funeral home, which

---

[26] Bible Hubcom, https://biblehub.com/lexicon/philippians/1-3.htm

is nice. I don't want to minimize anyone who did this for me—it was a generous sign of their care for me. The spread of flowers we received was impressive and brightened up the room we spent many hours in over the course of a couple of difficult days. Sadly, flowers die after a week or so. I kept any cards that came with the flowers, and we were able to distribute the plants to various family members, which helped. However, there are many creative alternatives that you can consider giving your friend as a gift in their grief.

When Kevin died, our son was two years old. I had a special account set up at our bank, and supporters could send money to the bank in his name in lieu of flowers. The donation envelopes were provided at the funeral home so contributors could just put the money in and mail it in that envelope. With the donated money, an education account was started for my son, and it's grown tremendously over the last fourteen years. Many contributors wrote kind messages on the envelopes, which the bank saved for me, and they brought a smile to my face. If you can support a grieving person with young children in this way, please consider it, as it really does help in the long-term.

For those of you that like to have a tangible gift to hand over to the grieving person, there are lots of options.

Gift cards: Restaurants, home improvement stores, clothing stores, or general VISA/MC cards. Make sure the denomination is written somewhere on the card or receipt. Even a $15 gift card is helpful: it can allow them to indulge in a coffee, lunch, or a treat. It's never too late to do this, and in some ways, waiting for a few months may even be better. I had some friends that gave me gas or restaurant gift cards several times, spaced out over the course of several months. It really helped, not only the thought but the repeated generosity.

Cash: Some online donation sites end up taking a percentage of the donations, therefore giving direct cash, when safe to do so, is a good option. Writing a check is also appreciated, though it is getting less common. Give what you feel comfortable giving if it's a small or large amount. If you prefer to be anonymous, you can ask the grieving person to keep it between the two of you.

Outdoor Stepping-stones: Check Garden centers or online. There isn't any work to be done with this type of memorial: just set it down near a porch, walkway, or garden. There are also stepping-stone kits that you must make yourself. Yes, the grieving person could do this project with their child or on their own, but for some grieving people, they might feel overwhelmed at the thought of doing this. If you are close enough to the family and want to offer to do a project with them, that could be a possibility but be prepared to bring all the supplies and take care of everything to complete the project.

Tree: A long-lasting gift that is sentimental and meaningful is a tree. This is a gift which would involve the grieving person. Is there a type of tree they or the deceased person loved, or that reminds them of that person? Maybe it's a pine tree if you want very little maintenance, as the pine needles that fall can become mulch. An oak tree or maple tree will require raking in the fall but provide shade and beautiful fall leaves. Blossoming trees give hope in the spring and sweet-smelling buds that often bring joy. Whatever you and they decide on, make sure that you offer to also pick up the tree and help plant it. I would avoid expecting the grieving person to have prepared the hole and bring your own shovels, gloves, peat moss and bark as well. The grieving person may want to be involved in the process, or they might just want to stay back and admire it once it's finished. Be sure to let the person know what kind of maintenance it requires, offer to come by occasionally to do the maintenance. If it needs watering, do it. If it needs fertilizer, go ahead and do it. The last thing you want to happen is for the tree to die because the grieving person did not have the time or means to maintain it. This is not a gift to give and forget about. Take a picture of the tree planting crew in front of it. Our family received a gift certificate to a local nursery and purchased Kevin's favorite tree, a redbud. It was planted up north at the family cottage and when the purple flowers blossom in the spring, I can just hear Kevin commenting on "his purple trees." My son helped plant and water it, which was so precious.

Photo credit Bethany France

My friend Tonya's daughter, Brookelyn, tragically died the summer before going into fifth grade. In a gesture of support some of her classmates helped purchase a tree and had it planted behind her elementary school near the playground. The students also wrote notes to Brookelyn and buried them under the tree. What a symbol of strength and beauty that will hopefully greet children for years to come as they enter the school. Tonya has a photo of the children who helped plant the tree, standing in front of it and holding Brookelyn's photo in a frame. Then, the year when Brookelyn would have graduated from high school, some of the same classmates who originally planted the tree posed in front of it with their graduation gowns on. They were missing Brookelyn, of course, but it made Tonya feel like she was not forgotten.[27]

Photo credit Wendy Schlett

Brookelyn Elias 11/5/03-7/18/14
Photo credit Tonya Elias

Windchimes: I have a set of chimes that hang on our deck and when the wind blows, I hear their slight tunes and I smile. Even though hanging windchimes does not seem like an arduous task for most people, recall that for a grieving person, making any, simple or hard, decisions can be stressful. Deciding where to hang them and doing the actual hanging can be another task for them to do. If you can, include a note that offers to help them hang the chimes if

---

[27] Personal interview with author on December 1, 2022. Used with permission.

they'd like. To ensure the grieving person knows this is a genuine request, write down your phone number and your general availability to help. For example, "I am available any time after three. Please let me know if you need help hanging these chimes and I'm honored to help." The more specific your offer is, the more genuine the request seems. But, as with any gift, be sure to include the receipt in case they don't have a spot for them, already have some, or for whatever reason they may not use them.

Quilts or Teddy bears made from the loved one's clothing: Clearly, this gift is one that would require the grieving person to know about in advance, since this is a personal decision to part with clothing. This gift is an incredibly special way to use the loved ones' clothing and repurpose them. Many bereaved people do not want to part with their person's clothing for a while, and that is understandable. Clothing brings back memories of the person, whether it be a special occasion when it was worn or that the memories of the person wearing it are vivid. You might phrase this idea with, "When you are ready to consider going through their clothing." It took me years to be willing to give up Kevin's clothes, knowing they would be cut up, even for a great cause. Make absolutely sure you have permission to use clothing for this purpose.

Quilts are nice because they can incorporate parts of the clothing into the quilt or entire shirt fronts. My aunt crafted two quilts made from my husband's clothing, one for me and one for my son. These projects were extra detailed, as I was able to find a photo of my husband wearing each of the featured shirts on the quilt, so a photo image transferred onto material was quilted into the square featuring the shirt in the picture. It was a huge undertaking by the quilter but are some of the most treasured items I now own.

Quilt by Jackie VanAllsburg – photo credit Bethany France

One quilter, who goes by the business called "Back Pocket Design," makes tooth fairy pillows (featuring jean pockets) and "Mug rugs" (coasters) that can also include pieces of clothing. She also took the edging from a pair of jeans and crafted it into a Christmas tree shape for an ornament. I had her make two memory pillows, one for me (as shown in the picture) and one for my son using my late husband's jeans. See www.BackPocketDesign.com for more information.

Made by BackPocketDesign – photo credit Bethany France

An organization called Living Threads Ministry is also an option for turning a loved one's clothing into a quilt. The organization uses one hundred percent of the quilt proceeds to support Bible clubs located in the Kibera Slum of Kenya, where any child may come to receive physical, spiritual, and emotional support. This is a way to honor your person with a warming gift and contribute to a great cause. See www.livingthreadsministry.org for more information.

Teddy bears made from clothing can be an incredibly special gift, especially given to children who want something tangible to hug. They can have a patchwork design that incorporates multiple clothing items. This idea is useful for creating multiple bears for various family members, even if you have a limited number of clothing items to use. I've seen examples of each grandchild getting a Teddy bear from Grandpa's flannel shirts or from Grandma's aprons.

Pictures: If you have any pictures of the person who passed away, pass those onto your friend. You can put them on a flash drive, or email them, put one in a frame and the others in an envelope, text them, or if you have a bunch of them, consider making a photobook of them. Check photo sites such as Shutterfly, where, for a reasonable cost, you upload the photos and they put the book together for you. Even if you find pictures of the deceased person years after the loss, still pass them on to the surviving person; they will treasure them. Sometimes the photo is one that the grieving person has never seen or hasn't seen in a long time, which makes them even more grateful to receive it. I have aunts and cousins that have continued to send me pictures of Kevin—many of which I have not seen because they were from a time before I had met him. These are treasures.

Jewelry: The birthstone of the person who passed is a meaningful gift, in the form of a necklace, bracelet, or earrings. There are many options on the internet for personalizing jewelry with birthstones or names or initials for reasonable prices. A website called AngelsofGrace.com offers beautiful remembrance and awareness bracelets. During a really difficult time in my life, a cousin of mine gifted me a Pandora bracelet with three different colored gemstones. At a family gathering, she pulled me aside, so it was just us together, making it clear she wasn't doing this for any recognition or attention. She explained the meaning of the colors of the gemstones she chose, (faith, hope, love) which made the gift even more meaningful.

Tile/brick/bench dedicated: Some libraries or towns may have an option to memorialize a loved one. At my local library, it was an engraved wall tile. You could offer to provide this type of lasting gift.

Our local school education foundation offers the purchase of a brick where you can choose three lines of wording, and the engraved brick will be placed in an area near the football stadium. This was a fundraiser for the foundation but also gave the opportunity to honor a teacher or memorialize someone special. My son and I loved going to find "Dada's brick" when we were told it was in place, and we still visit it when we are in the area. Be sure to get the grieving person's permission before purchasing a memorial like this.

One church offered the purchase of engraved bench plaques that would be placed on benches surrounding the church. I had been saving up money to pay for the bench plaque, and a loving group of women from my church exercise group surprised me by covering the cost. Talk about tangibly blessing someone—these women accomplished that! Some nature parks or gardens have trail signs that are dedicated to someone who has passed away. These types of tributes not only honor the deceased person but may also provide a donation to the entity where it will be.

Story or poem: It's so important that the loved ones left behind hear about the impact their loved one had on others. They want to hear stories that they weren't familiar with or may have forgotten. I asked a co-worker of my late husband if he would write about his memories of my husband that I could give to my son someday. He was glad to, though he admitted it was hard since he was still in shock and grieving. Besides working together, he and Kevin had gone fishing, completed building projects, and had become good friends. He managed to write several pages. He wrote about Kevin's work ethic and the valuable ideas he brought to the job.

One story he mentioned was the day my husband came into work and announced that I was pregnant with our son and how happy he was, grinning from ear to ear. I know my son will treasure these pages. What a gift that you can provide to a grieving person.

Books: I have listed a few titles in the resources section that I found helpful. You can write on the inside cover if you choose to make it personal. The books on grief that I received, I'll be honest, I did not read for quite a while. I felt that if I had any free time, I generally wanted it to not be grief-related but a distraction from the grief I was immersed in. There are some great grief books out there; just be aware it might take time before the grieving person decides to pick them up and read them. The grief-related books for my son I read right away, and we re-read them many times.

Magnets/bookmarks: Don't underestimate the thoughtfulness of these. There are many I've seen that have a verse on them, or poem, that I've kept in my car, purse, refrigerator—even on the dryer. They are little tidbits of wisdom that can help a grieving person have a little bit brighter day or moment.

Photography Gift certificates: At some point, the family may be ready for photos. There are many small business photographers who would be glad to provide this service for a family who has recently been through a tragedy and is trying to focus on the family that they have left. Be sure that your gift certificate is enough to pay for the session and that at least some photos are included. If the recipient wants more, they can order more, but it's not a good idea to cover only some of the service and put the recipient in a position where they must come up with the rest. One such photo session I did after my husband died included several poses of my son and me and a few with us together holding a photo of Kevin.

Salon Services Gift certificates: This could be providing a relaxing service for the recipient that they might see as a luxury and not want to spend money on. If they have young children, offering to watch their children while they use the certificate is a bonus. In times of tragedy, expenses like this might not be top priority due to finances or other obligations but not having to pay for these services might make them easier to schedule and enjoy.

Christmas Ornaments: Caution: the grieving person does not want to receive twenty ornaments that say, "There's a new angel in Heaven this year." However, there are some thoughtful ornaments that remind us of the person that died: his favorite sports team or hobby, a picture of her in a framed ornament, or a simple angel. Include a note with this ornament that says you were thinking of your loved one (say the person's name) and wanted them (the recipient) to know that you think about the person often and miss and love him or her. There are ornaments for just about everything you can imagine, so there are plenty of options here. One of my favorite ornaments received was of a little bunny on a swing with a big smile on his face. I had told a friend about how my two-year old son was swinging at the park one day. With a big smile on his face, his eyes were closed, and he was looking upward toward the bright sun. He said he was trying his hardest to swing high enough to reach Heaven so he could see his dada. While it broke my heart, I will never forget that innocent and precious image. The fact that my friend remembered this story I'd told her and thought of my son when she saw it and then bought the ornament was very touching.

Cards: Most people may not consider a card a gift, but it can be. If you take the time to send a card, make sure to write an encouraging message inside. Tell a funny story about the person who died or what impact they had on you and what you'll remember most about them. If you're sending the card to a person going through a difficult time, tell them you are thinking about them and will continue to pray for them (and really do that). There are many available cards nowadays; it can be a simple "thinking of you" card. I recently picked up a card that simply says on the outside, "This sucks. I am sorry." Then on the inside, you can elaborate or empathize or promise to be there for them.

Providing essential supplies: I had a generous friend contact me when she found out I was pregnant after my second tragedy and asked which type of diapers I preferred to use. She offered to send me a large box of diapers each month for a year and would check in every now and then to see if I needed a different size. I was blown away by this kindness, and it was very much appreciated. Every month when I saw the box on my porch, I felt loved and taken care of. There are so many options, like these, critical supplies that are so helpful.

Cautions About Tangible Gifts

Remember that it is the thought that counts... followed by some action that really makes a difference. The idea that you want to give a grieving person something to hold, something to read, something to use is a nice gesture. Make sure that you are not buying something with the intention to then check this off your list: "Buy item for grieving friend—check," and then consider that your support role has been completed. Grieving people *like* gestures and gifts, but what they *need* is support. Please go ahead and consider these ideas but don't let it take the place of emotional support—consistent and genuine for the long-term.

If Assembly Required, Consider Assembling

One of the best gifts I received on the first Christmas without my husband was for my son, but it blessed me as well. Good friends gave my son his first bike for his birthday. That "Gravel Blaster" brought such a smile to my son's face when he saw it. The even better part of the gift, for me, was that my friends assembled the bike for me right then and there. This was really an important factor in how awesome this gift was. Being a single mom with so many additional responsibilities now, the "assembly required" signs are dreadful. It's not that I can't do it in most cases, but it is a treat when others offer to do it as part of the gift. Keep this in mind when giving gifts that require work or assembly before they can be used. If you can at least offer to assemble it, go ahead and assemble it, especially a gift that the recipient likely will want to use right away. Or, set up a time soon to assemble it for them—and keep your word. If they say no thank you, still try to check in and see if they've changed their mind and want help with it. If the child is at an age where they might like to help assemble it, you could offer to do that with them. Even a toddler might like to hold parts and help turn a screwdriver, for example.

Intangible alternative gifts

The following list includes some service/support ideas that can be just as or even more meaningful than a tangible gift:

Charity Golf Outings/Charity Runs & Rides: For five years after the death of my husband, his godfather Paul, organized a golf scramble to not only remember Kevin but also raise funds for our son's education. It was a lot of work to execute but what a blessing. It made me feel so loved that friends and family would donate their time and resources to support us. Similarly, two young widows I know were blessed by a charity run and a memorial bike ride in honor of their late husbands, with the funds benefiting their children's educational accounts. If you can participate in such events, it will positively impact the surviving family members so that their loved ones are not forgotten.

If you want to organize such an event, make sure the grieving person has given permission and wants to be a part of it. However, don't require them to oversee it or have too much responsibility with it. The event could be very emotional and overwhelming, and you need to make sure to give grace and understanding because of the impact it could have. Don't be afraid of organizing such an event but pray and gather a team of helpers to make it successful.

T-shirt support: Examples I've seen: Ezra Strong, Shelly's Joy Squad, Moody Blues, Pray for Payton: these can be ordered online for a reasonable price. Be sure to check with the family to make sure they approve of the idea and message. You could consider pricing the shirt such that a portion is donated to the family or to a charitable cause. My friend's son Ezra, who was battling cancer, seeing his classmates, teachers, friends, and family wear "Ezra Strong" T-shirts made him feel supported and loved.

One elementary school organized a "pay to wear a hat" day, and the money collected purchased toys for a child going through cancer treatment. One caveat of this idea is to make sure it doesn't overwhelm the child or their family or leave out the other children in the household. The family may be limited by space to store the toys, or the child could simply receive an overabundance of toys and games. I recommend establishing a backup plan once the initial goal is reached. Maybe that includes the remaining funds being donated to a charity that the child is passionate about, gift cards for the family, buying new playground equipment for the school, or setting up a scholarship in their honor.

One child experienced joy and excitement as he headed home from treatment to find his driveway decorated with chalk drawings and messages. It turns out his teachers had organized and executed this, also bringing cards signed by the students that they had delivered to the house. These chalk drawings may have been temporarily visible celebrations, but they will be remembered for a long time and were impactful.

Lawn/yard work. At the visitation of my husband's funeral, a friend came up to me and said her husband really loved to mow the lawn, and she would like to arrange to have him mow for the rest of the summer. She said, "Really. I'm serious – it's no trouble at all." Not only did she mean it, but she followed up with me and set it up. Her husband was not just "voluntold" but reiterated to me that he enjoyed helping in this way. He would show up each week, head to the shed, and mow with a friendly wave and smile. Sometimes I wouldn't be home, but other times I would be outside playing with my son. At times, I felt bad because I was home and capable of mowing the lawn myself. But, I learned to let myself be cared for and be able to focus on what no one else could: being mom. Years later, after my second tragedy, once again, I had a friend reach out and ask if I mowed the lawn myself. I admitted that yes, it was tricky with an eight-year-old and a five-month-old. I referred to my lawn as a "mullet lawn," since it was often short in the front and long in the back since I couldn't accomplish both at the same time. Once my friend heard this, she arranged for her husband, and sometimes their kids, to mow my lawn that summer. Again, it was such a blessing to not have to worry about this task. Don't underestimate the support in the form of yard work.

One neighborhood surprised a new widow with hanging up outdoor Christmas lights following the sudden death of her spouse. It was a way for the neighbors to help bring literal light to her life during a hard time.

One early spring, I opened my garage door to find a neighbor and her daughters weeding my front walk. I hadn't planned to plant flowers that year, as I didn't have the energy to weed and plant. This neighbor was startled to see me because she didn't think I was home. I was floored not only by the generous help with weeding, but even more so that she intended to do it without me knowing it was her—she didn't want recognition. What a nice example to set for her kids too. Guess what: I planted flowers after that.

Cleaning, shopping or errand services. While this is not a tangible gift to hand over to the grieving or struggling person, the action of taking a task off their plate is. If you feel led to help—be specific. Maybe you offer that your normal shopping day is Sunday, and you're glad to pick up whatever groceries they need—they can think about it, and you'll reach out the night before and see if they've thought of anything. They can respond to your reach-out text with a list, and you can deliver at about six o'clock. Ask if that time frame would work for them and be flexible if there's a better time that works. Another idea is cleaning or doing laundry. It's often easier to clean when it's not your house—it goes quicker because you are not stopping to organize—you're just cleaning. If you can spare a couple of hours, you could offer to clean for them—even just dusting/vacuuming, tidying up the kitchen, sweeping, and emptying the trash are blessings to a tired, grieving person. Piled-up laundry can also be a relatively easy task to help with if your friend will accept the offer of help. Any other offers of running to the post office or picking up dry cleaning or supplies, or taking family members to appointments could make a big impact.

Be gentle so as not to insinuate that they are not keeping up with household tasks, but that it is a way for you to take something off their to-do list. One of Kevin's good friends and his wife lived several states away, but they decided to pay for several months of housecleaning for us from a cleaning service. Grieving people have a hard time keeping up with chores when they are sad, overwhelmed, and not feeling well. Looking at the household chore list can lead to feeling depressed and overwhelmed.

Don't underestimate the intangible gift. The power of the offer, follow-through, and consistent, ongoing support is critical. Be specific and genuine. The main goal is to relieve stress from the grieving or struggling person and, in doing so, show your care and support. I'm not downplaying the special tangible gifts that are thoughtful, but it's important to consider alternatives like service gifts. They aren't as quick or convenient for the giver, but they could be more long-lasting and impactful. Truly helping a grieving friend isn't just a one-time checkmark off your "should do" list. It takes time and effort, but I promise you it's worth it and appreciated.

Gwen

The gifts you give, either tangible or intangible, are an important part of what God uses to show love to the bereaved. When pain interrupts our lives and severs our ability to believe God has any ongoing interest in us, that is when others come into the story. God uses His people who are showing love through gifts or acts of service to remind His children that He is there, providing and showing His love and care. I want to encourage you when someone comes to your mind, act on that. Reach out, send a card, buy a candy bar, and leave a note that says, "You are loved, you are prayed for," and then ask God to use it for His purpose. He knows the heart and needs of your hurting friend; you are the hands and feet (and pocketbook) He uses to meet their needs. Don't let fear or worry that a gift, card, or thought is too small keep you from acting on what was laid on your heart. Send a text when they come into your mind that says, "Be strong and courageous," "How is your strength today?"

or "You are doing a great job" displays the life-giving power of friendship.

The gifts I am about to mention have been woven into this entire book, but I would like to give them their own space here.

Gift of a non-anxious spirit

Take the time to calm yourself if you feel overwhelmed by the task of supporting your friend. If seeing someone's pain is hard, that is normal, but you can give the gift to them and yourself by asking the Holy Spirit to calm you. You can admit that you are scared and unsure, and they will appreciate your authenticity. Trust me, I have done it many times. Calm is just as contagious as panic so if you want them to be calm, you must be calm. It is not a bad idea to take time to catch your breath after spending time with them. It is also not a bad idea to take a break from your friend, if needed. If you had a vacation planned while your friend is experiencing loss, it could be that you can still go (depending on many factors here, I think you can figure that out). But my point is, if when you return you are more rested and non-anxious, that will serve you both even more. Remember, you cannot pour from an empty cup.

Gift of Understanding

Being sympathetically aware of other people's feelings, tolerant, and forgiving is the definition of understanding, according to Oxford Languages.[28] Give this freely. Awareness, tolerance,

---

[28] https://www.google.com/search?q=understanding+definition&rlz=1C1CHBF_enUS919US919&oq=understanding+de&gs_lcrp=EgZjaHJvbWUqCggAEAAYsQM YgAQyCggAEAAYsQMYgAQyDAgBEAAYFBiHAhiABDIGCAIQRRg5M g0IAxAuGIMBGGLEDGIAEMgcIBBAAGIAEMgcIBRAAGIAEMgYIBhBFGE EyBggHEEUYPNIBCDcxMDBqMWo3qAIAsAIA&sourceid=chrome&ie=UTF-8

---

and forgiveness: what a great combination to bring to the table. What more could a friend ask for? My husband is a great driver, especially in bad weather or traffic. Me, not so much. I began to look at the difference in us, and it seems he understands what is needed most in those situations. His awareness is that you must slow down, so he is never in a hurry. He has forgiveness for others and how they move in and out of traffic, not fretting over what others are doing. He is so tolerant of interruptions in life or how he wants things to go. The good news here is that I have mastered these skills in relationships and in my work with the bereaved. I am not attached to the outcome of how I think people need to grieve or where they need to be on any given day, but to allow them to lead the way and teach me. It is a gift. You can give too.

The Gift of Laughter

Proverbs 17:22: "A joyful heart is good medicine, but a broken spirit dries up the bones." Laughter is good for us! I have heard that a child laughs 200-300 times a day on average while an adult laughs only 15 times each day. Clearly, children laugh way more than adults do, but life is a strange mixture of joy and sorrow. People often feel guilty that they are not honoring the person who died if they express joy. Laughter is good for our minds and bodies, making it an important part of caring for ourselves. Scientific studies have shown that laughing lowers blood pressure and reduces stress hormones. It increases the circulation of antibodies in the bloodstream and makes us more resistant to infection. Laughter is a stress reliever, a pain reducer, strengthens our immune function, and has many other benefits according to the Mayo Clinic.[29]

---

[29] Stress Relief from Laughter? It is No Joke, Mayoclinic.org, September 22, 2023, https://www.mayoclinic.org/healthy-lifestyle/stress-management/in-depth/stress-relief/art-20044456

Laughter is good for our entire well-being. It is life-giving and good for our souls.

Laughter is just as much a release of emotions as crying; they both relieve a lot of pressure. Therefore, it is okay to laugh with your grieving friend. Now, I am not talking about arriving at their home and reading from a 101-joke book. I am talking about when something is funny, share it. When they laugh, laugh along. If they need comic relief, ask them what that looks like to them and find a way to make it happen. Maybe for some, it is a comedy show, but be sure to ask them and if they do not feel like going, be okay with that. And do not get upset if they are "no fun" for a time. (And don't point that out to them—keep it to yourself!) Bereaved people do often have anhedonia: the inability to feel pleasure. It is a real thing and is usually temporary; the joy does return over time. Don't be afraid to introduce laughter and joy to them; just pay attention to their reaction in case it is not comfortable for them yet or at that moment.

A few other things families have expressed over the years to me are how much gifts mean to them and the expression of love and remembrance. The stories and memories shared, both good and sometimes painful, are treasures for sure. It is important for them to know that their person is not forgotten, and these gifts and acts of service show that. With that in mind, a gift down the road after some time has passed, or it is near a holiday or special day, is just as meaningful: so, it is okay to wait.

Another piece of advice about gifts that grievers have shared is they can feel obligated to keep and display them all. It can be overwhelming to have a yard/deck full of chimes, memory stones, bird houses, and the like. Be sure to include receipts and permission to return gifts if they are not used, multiples are given, or for any reason the person has. If you don't know what to give, ask a bereaved person (not the one you are currently supporting but someone further down the road), "What gifts meant the most to you?" Or, if you yourself have experience, think back to what touched you or was particularly helpful.

Lastly, how I wish I could take the pressure of the "thank you" note off the bereaved person's to-do list. So, I ask you to add the "no need for a thank you note" to your gift. Although I know the obligation to send it will still be there, I wish I could take that away because many of my bereaved clients share with me that there is a heaviness to complete the "thank-yous." On top of everything else going on in their lives, you can help decrease that pressure by not expecting one and explicitly telling them one is not necessary. That would be a blessing. If they insist on writing a thank-you note, offer to help. They may want to write it, but you can address envelopes, add stamps, or help in any part of the process.

 ## Quick Tips

- Cash and gift cards, without any expectation of when/how they should be used. Trust that they will be used for good purposes by the grieving person/family.
- Pictures of the person who died—don't assume the grieving person already has the picture.
- It is thoughtful to include a personalized note with your gift.
- Any way to memorialize the person—trees, plaques, benches.
- Books about grief—know that the grieving person may not read them for a while.
- Memorial events—help organize them, or support/attend them, and check on the grieving person days after the event.
- Cards, notes, texts, calls, personal reach-outs (intention and often) are true gifts.

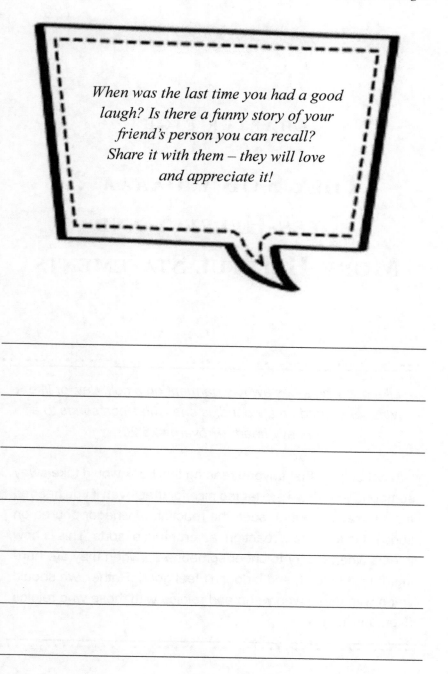

When was the last time you had a good laugh? Is there a funny story of your friend's person you can recall? Share it with them – they will love and appreciate it!

_____

_____

_____

_____

_____

_____

CHAPTER EIGHT

THEY SAID WHAAAAT? LESS-HELPFUL AND MORE-HELPFUL STATEMENTS

• •

Like one who takes away a garment on a cold day, or like vinegar poured on a wound, is one who sings songs to a heavy heart. (Proverbs 25:20)

I do not believe that anyone reading this book would take away someone's coat; we are far too nice for that, even if you needed a coat. Have you ever seen the reaction of vinegar poured on soda? It is an instant reaction, an eruption of sorts. This is how it feels when we try to cheer someone up when they are hurting. It isn't helpful, and it doesn't feel good. Rather, we should weep with those who weep and rejoice with those who rejoice (Romans 12:15).

• •

Bethany

Grieving people understand that most comments are meant to be helpful. Despite good intentions, it's common to hear unsolicited advice, ignorant questions or statements, and cliché phrases that aren't the best way to be supportive when someone is grieving a loss.

Before we go further, I don't want you to be discouraged after reading this chapter. It's possible that you've said these things in the past; I know I have. I still sometimes struggle to find the appropriate words in hard situations. Start now to understand the phrases to avoid, and you'll be a more supportive friend going forward. Most of the less-helpful phrases fall into one of five categories. After reading what to avoid saying, I'll offer a list of better phrases so we can learn how to approach this situation better. Tip: You might want a highlighter for this chapter! When we get to the "more helpful" phrases, highlight those that you can practice saying and have ready, those that sound more comfortable for you.

Less-Helpful

1. Trying to find the positive in an awful situation.

When someone is deep in grief, asking them to find the bright side can be a turn-off. I understand the desire to give a glimpse of hope to someone, but a grieving person doesn't want to be told how to feel or what to do. They want to be allowed to feel what they feel when they feel it and not be judged on it. There are moments when they may have thought about the bright side and/or tried to find the good in each day. With time, most grieving people can acknowledge blessings despite the loss. But it should be on their time, not at your request. The following are statements to avoid saying:

"Look at the bright side": One grieving mom who had a miscarriage had someone tell her stories about disabled children, implying that had the pregnancy continued, it might have resulted in the baby being disabled. This was a head-shaker to this newly grieving mom.

"You're lucky that...": I once had a dear friend vent her frustration about an argument she was having with her husband regarding which paint color to choose for their dining room. She then said to me, "You are so lucky you don't have to argue about paint colors with your husband." What I thought to myself was that I would give *anything* to argue with my husband about paint colors right now if he were just able to be here with me.

"You're still young": And ... I have time to find another husband? Or, in the case of a child that died, I have time to have more kids? The last thing on a grieving person's mind is filling the void. We don't want "another" to replace the person; it's impossible anyway.

"At least it wasn't...": Grieving people often are told how it could have been worse. The worst is true: the person died. The results are in. The marriage is officially over. The fact that there remain one or two things that could have made this tragedy even worse isn't very encouraging.

"At least they didn't suffer...": We can all agree we don't want anyone to suffer. Whether a person dies slowly or quickly is not what a grieving person wants to think about.

"He/she looks good…": Please. They look dead. Enough said.

"They're in a better place": As Christians, we know that if they believed that Jesus Christ was their Lord and Savior that they are now in Heaven, pain-free and happy. But a newly grieving person might believe "here and alive" is a better place.

I was haunted for years by a situation that happened within hours of Kevin dying. A religious leader was quickly called to my house. The immediate family was gathered in a circle of prayer in my living room. The world had stopped turning for us, and we were in shock. In a tense moment of holding hands, while we hoped to hear some sort of comforting words, I became livid. The leader said that even if Kevin could come back right now, he wouldn't. Screech! (The worst sound of brakes squealing that you've ever heard.) I was shaking and trying to hold it together, but this man kept going on about how Kevin wouldn't turn back to Earth, even if he could; Heaven is that amazing. The flustered thoughts in my mind were that of course he would come back! He would see us all miserable and crying; he would hear his confused dogs barking. Kevin would see his two-year old son at the neighbor's house, who was asking when he was going back home. Kevin would come running back to us all. But I said nothing, as I was too mad to even speak. Even years after my loss, I can say this was a very inappropriate and insensitive thing to say at such an early moment to a new widow.

"I never liked him/her anyway": I wish I was kidding, but this was really spoken to a grieving person in a death situation and in a divorce situation to someone else. While it's possible that the deceased person was not a kind or good person in your eyes, the grieving person still has suffered a loss and likely did not ask your opinion of the person. There may be some relief by the grieving person if the deceased was mean, made bad choices, or caused a lot of pain upon others. Perhaps the person who died was an ex-husband or ex-family member for good reason. You might not understand it, but grief is complicated. It's not helpful to point out the deceased person's faults.

2. Giving Unsolicited Advice

You may have great advice to give, but grieving people don't want to be told what to do. You can let them know that if they ever have questions about a specific topic that you are glad to give them information. They are facing a lot of decisions, and they don't need the added pressure of what you think they need to do. The phrase "you need to" or "you should" is very pushy. Here are some common unsolicited pieces of advice to avoid:

"You need to sell your house/his car/that boat/RV": You might be concerned about added expenses and responsibilities that death brings about. It is expected that some adjustments will need to be made. If there is only one driver in the house now, it might be wise to sell a vehicle. If the survivor didn't really enjoy using the RV, it might be a good idea to sell it ... at some point. These are tough decisions that only the owner/surviving spouse can make. It can be hard to part with belongings, but in some cases it's a necessity. However, I advise caution in pressuring a grieving person to sell or give away anything, letting them decide instead.

"You need to get back to work/school": There comes a time to start moving forward, get back into a routine, and find some sort of "new normal." But directing them to do that on your time, not theirs, is not helpful.

"You should see a therapist" or "You should get on some meds": If you are concerned that your friend is not taking care of themselves well or is struggling, be gentle. Make it clear that your concern comes from love, not judgment or hope that they will "get over" the loss quicker. If you have experience with a grief counselor or recommend a great doctor, thoughtfully provide the grieving person with the information for their consideration.

Various medical advice: One woman who had a miscarriage due to an ectopic pregnancy had a nurse friend try and console her. The nurse friend decided to explain that some women don't ovulate with both fallopian tubes so it's possible that she may never conceive again. This conversation was very damaging. To let her know that not only did she lose this one, but she may never conceive again, was inappropriate and mean, really. While the grieving mom wanted to learn more about what her future might hold with her health and the ability to have more children, give her a minute. When the time is right, she can ask her doctor for his or her honest opinion. One widow was also advised that she should not go on any medication and just work through the grief. Again, this is not helpful because that is between the bereaved and her doctor and there are many circumstances others may not be aware of.

3. Nosey questions

Before you ask questions, ask yourself why you want to know. Is it so you can be helpful and try to fill a need? Or is it because you are curious? Sometimes the motivation is that we want to be "in the know" and be the source of information. Our brains may want to make a judgment about the loss—was it expected, was it preventable, could it happen to us? We don't want to make the grieving person feel like there is something more they could have done to prevent the loss, prepare better, or change the outcome. They may be questioning themselves on this anyway and don't need reinforcement of their insecurity. We don't always have bad intentions when we ask nosey questions; it is human nature to be curious. But before asking, think, *Why do I want to know this?*

"Did he/she have life insurance?" "Will you have to go back to work?" "Are you ok financially?": It is natural to be concerned about a grieving person's financial situation. Especially if the loss was a person who provided the main support or childcare or care of the home. Now a surviving spouse may need to pay for help in these areas. Funerals are expensive, and being genuinely concerned is valid. However, it is up to the grieving person how much information they want to divulge and to whom. I had a friend ask me if my spouse's life insurance was enough to pay off my mortgage. I quickly responded that it was nowhere close to that. The question prompted me to feel ashamed that even though we had tried, we did not get approved for more life insurance, other than a year's salary. I felt bad about myself for several days, which didn't help, wondering if we should have done more to prepare for this unforeseen event.

Another example of nosey questions is when I once had a twelve-year-old boy and his mom over for dinner, and he bluntly asked me if I received any money from my husband's life insurance and how I was able to afford things. I nearly choked on my food, especially because his mom didn't say a word to stop him or apologize on his behalf. She just sat there like she, too, was waiting for the answer. I stammered as best I could that there were some benefits available from the government in certain situations, and sometimes life insurance is available. I felt very uncomfortable answering this question, but since it was a curious child, I tried as best I could to respond. By asking these questions, I'm sure you're hoping for good news but realize it may make the person uncomfortable and even judged.

4. Religious

"Heaven/God needed another angel": It's a nice image. However, God doesn't need people to die so that He can use them for something there. When I explained to my two-year-old that his "Dada" died, I unintentionally blamed God. I said that God needed Kevin's help because he was so talented at doing so many things. At the time, I thought it was a good idea, and I did the best I could under the circumstances. But that led my son to sometimes blame God for His dad's death, and that wasn't my desire for him. A short time later, I explained truthfully that his heart stopped working properly, a concept he understood even at age three. It's nice to think of dying as getting the ultimate promotion to angel, but it's not the best phrase to offer a grieving person, especially a child.

"Everything happens for a reason": A common reaction to loss is, "Why did this happen?" If you respond with the "reason" phrase, are you ready to answer when they ask what that reason is? Or is that when you awkwardly pat them on the shoulder and find a quick excuse to scoot away? A grieving person may find it hard to conclude that their loss happened for a good, unknown "reason." Especially for recent grief, they can't see too far down the road. Those that have worked through their grief may be able to see blessings even following the loss. God has a plan, indeed, for everyone's life, but in times of pain, it is hard to understand. Best to avoid this cliché phrase.

Religious passages: Know your audience. If you know they are Christ-followers, it can be appropriate and helpful to share if they are heartfelt. If you are not sure, general reassurance of peace and comfort might be best. You can always offer to pray with someone but do not be offended if they decline or act unsure. If they act uncomfortable, say a brief prayer, and move on. If they decline for you to pray with them, you can always let them know you'll be praying for them, which is not putting them on the spot. You can always plant a seed about faith in God but try not to evangelize someone who is amid tragedy, as it may turn them off to you and God. They may be open to it at some point so you can bring it up from time to time, but don't overwhelm them and be sure to look for clues about their discomfort. Even some faith-filled Christians who are grieving aren't always in the mood to hear scripture.

"God won't give you more than you can handle": When a person is grieving, they feel they can't handle much at all. It's all so overwhelming: getting dressed, attending the funeral, making dinner, or dealing with another phone call or filling out tedious paperwork. They can't handle a rigorous work schedule or doing tasks that they found so simple before their loss. Have you heard of people who have one tragedy or loss after the other? First this happens, then another loss, then another obstacle, then something else. So, does God just keep piling up more on them because he knows their "handle limit" and He won't surpass that? I've learned to personally interpret this phrase as "God won't give you more than you can handle *on your own.* You need people, and you need Him." If you are tempted to use the "handle" phrase, consider adding the "on your own" words and follow it with promises."God will be with you every step and so will I" (and really be there).

5. Common phrases meant to be helpful – but aren't.

Before you speak these phrases, think first about the motivation behind them.

"Let me know if you need anything": The most common phrase I've heard; I know I've said it many times, before and after my own grief journey. I must consciously try not to say it. After my first loss, if someone offered this to me, my gut reaction was to reply, "I need my husband back. Can you do that?" I never actually said it out loud, but I thought it. If you offer this, the grieving person will probably not let you know. Besides that, they don't know what they need, or they need so many things they don't know where to start. The phrase itself sounds somewhat helpful but often time passes, and the person predictably never lets you know. That probably means they are ok, right? They've got other people helping them must be the case. If you offer this phrase, are you ready to react to their need if they do reach out? What if they reach out with the "anything," and it's not something you are willing or able to do? Another reason I'm not a fan of this phrase is that you've now put the burden on the grieving person to reach out to you.

"I know how you feel": Maybe a little bit. Maybe you have suffered a tragic loss and can empathize with what they are going through. But not exactly. Telling someone you know how they feel will likely evoke an automatic thought or response of "No, you don't." They don't want to compare losses with you right now. The type of loss, cause of death, the nature of the relationship, age, financial situations, and many other factors make their grief uniquely theirs. And please, for the love of everything holy, if you're trying to help the grieving person not feel so alone, do not compare a human death to a pet's death. I had to say goodbye to two of Kevin's best canine friends not long after he died, and it was awful. But please do not say that you know how a widow feels because you recently had to say goodbye to Fluffy, no matter how hard that was for you.

"How are you?" (Hoping they say "great!"/not wanting them to be brutally honest): This one is tricky. If you ask it while you are rolling your shopping cart past them, you're not going to likely get an honest answer, and your question won't seem genuine. Your body language might also indicate that you are asking the question but don't really want an honest answer, if they're not having a good day or are struggling. If you are expecting them to say they are, "great," but they say anything but "great," how will you respond? Be genuine in asking and be prepared for whatever answer might come out. Be willing to listen and respond with empathy.

"You're so strong": This is an intended compliment and some-times when this was said to me, it made me feel empowered. But the truth is most feel they *have* to be strong. There's no choice in the matter—they must be strong for other children, other family members, staff, or decisions that depend on them. Another reason a grieving person might appear strong is because they have their moments—and when you see them "being strong," they are having a good moment. The danger, though, in telling a grieving person that they are "so strong" is that you've made a decision about how they are, and the grieving person now feels they have a reputation to uphold. They may think *I cannot let them see me cry, I cannot admit that I need help, or I'm not ok.* Michelle Steinke-Baumgard, author of *Healthy Healing* and founder of One Fit Widow, points out that well-intentioned supporters "don't realize the weight those words carry and that we place that weight squarely on our shoul-ders as an added responsibility."[30]

More Helpful (Grab the highlighter!)

Try your best to say what is in your heart but also put thought into it before saying it. Don't be afraid to say the wrong thing, just practice. When you see them, say something. If it comes out wrong, quickly say, "I'm sorry. I don't know what to say other than

---

[30] Michelle Steinke-Baumgard, *Healthy Healing* (New York: HarperOne, 2017), p.22.

I care about you, and I am thinking about you." Avoid cliches and make your words genuine and specific.

Regarding the "bright side" —rephrase it into an "I am thankful . . ."—so it is the speaker looking at the bright side, not the grieving person being expected to.

"I'm thankful for the first responders and medical care."

"I'm thankful for the love you gave them."

"I'm thankful he was safe at home and not driving."

"I'm thankful for the years you had with them, even though it wasn't enough."

Regarding what to say at the funeral/viewing:

"I loved his eyes—they were such a pretty blue."

"I loved her smile; I will always remember that."

"I haven't seen him in years, but I will always remember the way he laughed . . ."

"She had such pretty hair."

Regarding their personal items that they might sell:

"If you get to a point where you think you want or need to sell something, I'd be glad to help you or recommend someone that will help you with it." (You surely don't want to see your grieving friend being taken advantage of or swindled or pressured into a bad deal). If it's you who wants the items, be extra gentle. Make sure to say, "If you ever get to a point where you want or need to sell something, I'd be honored to get the chance to own something from that person, and I'd take good care of it." Don't expect a "sweet deal" or it to be a gift to you. If that does end up happening, and you buy something that was previously the deceased person's item, follow up with the grieving person and let them know how much it means to you, that you are enjoying the item and think of their person when you use it.

Regarding your care & concern:

"I think of you a lot. I care about you and am always concerned about how you are doing. I have some resources here that I want to share with you that I found helpful to me. Feel free to use them if you want to. This is so hard, and I hope you know you're not alone. There is help out there for everyone."

"I hope your work is being good to you/understanding of your situation."

"This must be so hard. I've heard it's good to try and get back to some sort of routine, even though it will be challenging and not the same."

"It won't be this painful forever, I promise. And I'll stick with you."

Regarding financial & insurance matters:

"If you need help contacting a life insurance company, I'd be glad to call or gather paperwork for you if that would help (without prying for information)."

"If you have any life insurance questions, I know an agent— let me know if you want their information."

"If you need any financial assistance, please reach out. I'll keep it confidential, but I know of some sources of support … or I can send you the information and you can contact them if you ever need to."

"I'd like to help you financially." (Consider starting with a certain amount and let them know if they need more, you are willing to help more, and you'll offer again.)

"I'm not sure what kind of situation you are in, and that's your business, but I want to help if you need it. Please accept (whatever amount you are comfortable with and leave it at that)."

"I'm glad to help you more if it's needed; please let me know if there is a specific need with gas cards, childcare, meal gift cards, or something different." (No one is likely to turn down cash or gift cards that you send them, but they will be hesitant to reach out and ask.)

Offer a few times if they've not taken you up on it previously. They might not feel comfortable accepting it at first, or their need for help might evolve as time goes on. I can't see anyone being offended by receiving money if there are no strings (expectations) attached. If it's too much, they will let you know. But there are so many unexpected expenses, it's not likely to be too much.

Regarding religious sentiments:

"I'm thankful for a place like Heaven, where I can't wait to give them a hug again."

"Even though I wish they were still here, I am grateful for Heaven."

"We will understand God's plan in time, even if we don't right now."

"I am so sorry this happened, but God is always with us."

"I am not sure where you are at in terms of faith in God, but I just want you to know that God loves you and He cares for you."

"My faith helped me through my own losses and struggles. If you ever want to know more about that, I would be happy to share."

"Is it ok if I pray for you?"

"God will provide for you—whether it's people, food, opportunities, support, help."

Regarding offers of help:

"I'd like to offer to bring you some meals (specific). I will reach back out to you (relieve them of the burden to reach out) on Wednesday (set specific expectations) and see what sounds good to you."

"I'm available every Wednesday evening, and I'll call you then to see if there is any way you've thought of where I can help."

"I go grocery shopping on Sundays, so I'll check in on Saturday night and see if I can bring you anything."

"Do you have lawn service? Is that something I can help you with? I can be there every Saturday in June and do that for you if you'd like."

"I'm one of those people that is here to help you."

"Here's my phone number. If you think of a need at some point, I'm just a text away. I'll be looking out for your number. I want to help."

Tip: If someone made a general offer to help, and I mustered up the bravery to reach out and ask, I would ask them up to two times. If they could not help either time, I typically did not ask again. If you can't help when they ask you, circle back soon if you are truly willing to help. Make it clear that you are good in your offer to help, and you will find the right time that works. Or assist them in finding someone who can be there when the person needs it.

If you've made that offer, "Let me know if you need anything," follow up with them–it's never too late. Let them know that you're still available to help if they have thought of anything. Tell them you truly want to help in some way. Offer to go for a walk or meet for coffee, no matter how much time has passed since you've made that offer.

Regarding experience with grief:

"I've been in a similar situation, and I just want you to know that I am here if you want a listening ear, shoulder to cry on, or want to talk about resources or support that helped me."

"For me, even though my situation was not quite the same, I found it helpful to get up at the same time each day and schedule things to do. It helped me start having some sort of routine. I know you'll find what works for you."

"I've known others who have had similar situations. If you want, I can research information for you and connect you with some support groups if you are interested."

"I have some background experience in this—if you ever want to talk or have questions, I'd be glad to spend some time with you."

Generally helpful words:

"I am so sorry:

    – for your loss

    – you are going through this

    – this happened

    – for the pain you are feeling

– you had to face that situation; that must have been really hard."

"There are no words/I don't know what to say, other than I am sorry for your loss."

"Life is hard. Really hard."

"How can I help?"

"I'm thinking of you and care about you/I think of you often."

"Grief affects people in different ways."

"Your loved one would be so proud of you."

"There is a purpose for the pain, but it's really hard to see and understand right now."

"You are not alone. I am with you."

"It's great to see you out and about. Isn't this weather beautiful? I saw your son the other day, and he is growing up so fast!" (Comments unrelated to the grief situation are not bad things either—they want to feel normal too.)

"I'm a good listener if you ever want to meet up for coffee (and reach out and invite them)."

"How are you doing today? How are you doing right now? How are you *really* doing—you can be honest."

"I admire how you've handled this really hard situation. I'm sure it's full of ups and downs."

"Can I ask what has helped you get through this? Your perseverance is inspiring."

"I don't know what to say. I care for you. I'm sorry for this tremendous loss. I want to help in any way I can or that you need."

Gwen

I am sure you are thinking about times you have said the "wrong" thing. I want you to forgive yourself. When we know better, we do better.

It is true that the bereaved extend much grace and forgiveness because they too remember that before this death happened to them, they had shared some of these cliché actions and statements as well. It is also true that many unhelpful or hurtful statements have caused them to sever relationships, leave churches/groups, or, at the very least, distance themselves from the person who said it. Why? Because it hurts. Because it minimizes and devalues their feelings. It is salt in the wound. We do not want to hurt people or push them away with things we say.

Why do these sayings come flying out of our mouths even when we know they are not helpful? Because we feel awkward, we want to help fix the pain, or we fear the heavy silence that follows when someone expresses raw emotions.

Behind most inappropriate behavior is fear. We fear silence; we fear looking like a fool who has no response; we fear the places their pain touches in our own hearts. It is a scary place to be. To *be*, that is the key. God created us as human *beings,* not as human doings. So, the most helpful thing we can do is not in what we say but rather in being in that space with them. Listen. Be slow to speak. In the book, *Don't Sing Songs to a Heavy Heart*, author Kenneth Haugk says, "You can use the quiet to pray silently for the hurting person and to ask for guidance in your caring. A perceptive pastor shared that he often prays these words: 'O Lord, please keep your arm around my shoulder and your hand over my mouth.' It goes on to say, "When silence fills the room, remember that God is beneath and within the silence, radiating His love. You can speak in love, you can listen in love, and you can simply be with the other person in love."[31]

During my time as a hospice social worker/bereavement coordinator, my role was to be an emotional support for the family as well as for the dying person. During that time, I learned so much from a mother of six who was dying. One day, when all her end-of-life tasks were done and death was quickly approaching, I found myself sitting many silent times with her in the living room. To be honest, there were times I wanted to leave because the silence was so heavy. More than that, I really wanted to do or say something to make this all better. On one of our last visits, she screamed out a heart-wrenching cry, "I don't want to die!" I can't tell you how long it was but during that time of silence that followed, my mind thought of things to say but none of them could make her pain not be pain. My eyes welled with tears, and I declared back, "I don't want you to die either." There was no doing, just being and relating.

[31] Kenneth C. Haugk, *Don't Sing Songs to a Heavy Heart: How to Relate to Those Who Are Suffering* (St. Louis, MO: Stephen Ministries, 2004), p.64.

 **QUICK TIPS**

- Be kind and genuine.
- Use phrases that are caring and helpful (not nosey or judgmental).
- If you realize you've said something inappropriate, apologize immediately.
- If you can't think of anything to say, rely on these:
  - I'm sorry you are going through this.
  - I think of you often.
  - I pray for you.
  - I wish I knew what to say to make it better.

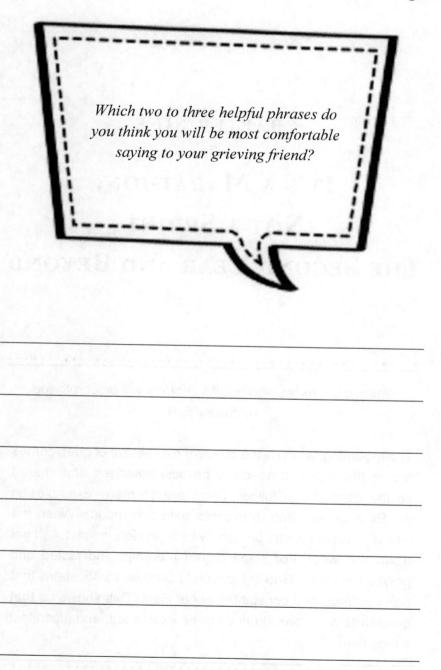

Which two to three helpful phrases do you think you will be most comfortable saying to your grieving friend?

_____

_____

_____

_____

_____

_____

CHAPTER NINE

IT'S A MARATHON, NOT A SPRINT THE SECOND YEAR AND BEYOND

· ·

Blessed are those who mourn, for they will be comforted.
(Matthew 5:4)

The mourning, which is the outward expression of grief, comes first in this verse. It needs to be acknowledged and shared so the comfort can follow. There are so many examples in the Bible of our need to express pain and mourn. When the wall of Jerusalem was broken, we see in Nehemiah 1:4, "I sat down and wept. For some days I mourned and fasted and prayed before the God of Heaven." I Samuel 15:35, states that Samuel "mourned constantly" about Saul. This shows us that our hearts will break; it needs to be expressed, and it can last a long time.

· ·

144

Bethany

Contrary to what you might think, many grieving people will tell you that year two, after a loss or death, is not easier. Michelle Steinke-Baumgard, who wrote *Healthy Healing,* explains the brutal and long-lasting numbness after her husband died in a plane crash. She said, "It's hard to explain to anyone who has not experienced the power of that kind of shock, but I was a shell of a human walking around, going through the motions for nearly an entire year. Once I did feel the pain, in many ways I wanted the shock to come back."[32]

I can relate to Michelle's experience, as can many people who go through such a hard loss. There was so much chaos (after both of my losses) that there was a lot to be done and decisions to be made; it was as if my body just didn't allow me to fully break down or feel emotions too completely. There were plenty of times of breakdowns, mostly in private, but the "autopilot" of shock just kept me moving most of the time, which probably came off as somewhat cold and strong. Don't be alarmed if a grieving person appears "too" strong—they may be hiding it well or may be in shock, and it will hit them at some point down the road—even a year or more later.

Even as I write this book, I still struggle with the "marathon vs sprint" with my care for others. When I recently heard about a friend who received a tough medical diagnosis, I "sprinted" into action. I went to the store and put together a bag of several items that would help her while receiving treatments. I dropped it off at her house within a week of finding out about her news. I've done a kind thing; I've been thoughtful; I've responded quickly; I've offered prayers, and anticipated needs and tried to fill those. I figuratively patted myself on the back and honestly thought, *Good*

---

[32] Michelle Steinke-Baumgard, *Healthy Healing* (New York: HarperOne, 2017), p.18.

job, self. It wasn't until a few days later that I shook my head in disbelief at my own fault. I am writing a book on how to support a grieving friend, and I've nearly checked my "good deeds" off a checklist for this friend. Her journey, and thus my support, is not over! This habit many of us have of checking tasks off our list is satisfying, but it does not apply when caring for our grieving friends. I am making an intentional effort to not only pray each morning when I walk by her house, but I check in consistently and let her know I am thinking of her and see if there are any current needs that I can help with. Her journey is long, and my support will be as well.

Continuing Support Through Events

Part of my friend Sharisse's healing process after the death of her eight-year-old son, Austin, involved putting together an event called "Austin's Art Party," near his birthday in April. She featured his artwork and set up creativity stations where kids could make their own masterpieces. The only "cost" to attend was to donate crayons, markers, pencils, and other art supplies, which she donated to a local children's hospital. Having friends continue to support, attend, and donate to this event showed Sharisse they hadn't forgotten him and wanted to honor his love of art while helping other children's hospital stays a little more bearable. If your friend has such an event, continuing to support it will mean a lot to your friend.

Another way that Sharisse was able to memorialize Austin was to have a "buddy bench" constructed and placed at the elementary school that he attended. This process involved her collecting an extensive number of plastic bottle caps that were donated to an organization that created the bench out of the plastic. By spreading the word among friends and family that there was a need for bottle caps, over the course of a year, the required amount was collected. Now this bench, dedicated in Austin's name, gives comfort to other kids who are feeling lonely and need a friend.

Photo credits
Sharisse Buchanan

Dean Austin Goodlin
4-11-2002 to 8-9-2010

My friend Tonya agrees, that of course the pain of losing a child endures well beyond a year.[33] There are all the "firsts," but also the seconds, the thirds, and the continual passing of time without her second-born child.

Tonya started a non-profit organization called Blessed by Brookelyn that is constantly providing help and support to people around the world. Ranging from providing backpacks and athletic equipment for children in need to providing food and clothing for the homeless and low-income families, to shipping loads of books to schools in poor communities, to raising money for a generator to be sent to an island devastated by a hurricane ... there is no end to the support Brooke's family gives in her honor. What is comforting to Tonya is that others are joining her in this mission to find joy in helping others, even when they are hurting. To support her causes is to support her as a bereaved mom.

---

[33] Personal interview with author on December 1, 2022, Used with permission.

Holidays, Change of Seasons, Milestones

Holidays are still hard for grieving people years later. If it weren't for my son, there is no way I would have set up a tree or put any decorations out for Christmas—the first or second or maybe even third year after the loss. For many grieving people, it is too much work with too much pain intertwined. In a season of struggling to act jolly, decorating the house is overwhelming. Some grieving people choose to leave town for holidays, so everything is different. If you stay home, and try to make things the same, you realize it is not going to be the same. There is an empty chair at the table. As their friend, you could offer to come over and help with decorations, making the task not so daunting. Consider offering for them to join you at your holiday gathering or offering to bring a meal to them. Offer to eat with them during the holidays so they are not alone. We shouldn't force them to celebrate certain things if they really aren't ready to, but they might take you up on your offer. Don't forget to check in with them—before, during, and after the holidays—to let them know you are thinking of them and see if there is a need you can help with or a way you can support them.

A married couple once called into a radio station on Valentine's Day and said they make it a point to buy a few cards for widows or widowers that they know instead of buying a card for each other. They were both widowed previously so they understand these overmarketed holidays that can bring pain to those who feel isolated during these holidays. You, too, can make it a point to send a card on a specific holiday every year to a grieving person. If you are going to spend money on a Mother's Day card, please consider buying an additional one if you are able. Send one to any of the following: a newly single mom (especially if her kids are too young to buy one themselves), or someone whose mom has passed away and tell them about a cherished memory you have of their mother, or anyone that you might think would have a difficult time on Mother's Day. Buying an extra card or two for these occasions is thoughtful and an unexpected blessing.

Remember that the "day of" is sometimes not as hard as the day leading up to, or the days afterward. The loneliness tends to set in *after* the event. There is typically support and anticipation leading up to the difficult event and then like a balloon popping, the support is gone, the calls stop, the confetti hits the floor, and the grieving person is left cleaning up the pieces. Please be the one to check on your friend several days or a week or weeks after an important event, like a holiday.

The change in seasons can affect grief each year. For me, even years after the death of my husband, the fall hunting season and the months leading to Christmas and my husband's birthday are hard. My husband was an avid hunter and recently for the first time, my son was able to go hunting with his grandpa. The wave of emotions I felt when we went up into the attic and went through several bins of hunting gear, knowing my son would wear some of his dad's clothes was exciting and a little sad. While it's been over a decade since his dad died, there are still, and will forever be, moments like this that bring back painful emotions. Your grieving friend, too, will experience their own reoccurrences of grief years later. The grief may not be as deep or last as long, but it can still be sad and lonely. Check in, let them know you are still thinking of them, and realize they may still have hard moments or days.

It's never too late to offer to fill in the gap, to reach out and recall a memory of that person or to offer support with a call, card, or gift. It's always appreciated. I still have relatives and friends reach out via text with a "Thinking of you," or "Happy birthday to Kevin in Heaven," or "I still remember his great laugh." Make a note of your friend's anniversaries and be diligent about reaching out.

For parents of children who are in Heaven, seeing photos of sporting events that their children were involved in can cause tears. Their child is not on that team, and they should be. The milestones: getting a driver's license, graduating, getting married, and having babies/grandbabies can force grief to resurface. I've struggled with "Father-Daughter" dances that some schools have. My daughter will not get to attend these events with her father, and it's heart-wrenching. I see photos of couples celebrating their anniversaries and know my spouse Kevin and I will not be jetting off to the Bahamas—we only made it to our eight-year anniversary. What is the best response you can provide when you see a grieving person struggling with these thoughts? Say, "I'm sorry. This stinks. I love you. I am here for you." Just don't step back; step alongside them so they aren't alone.

In time, families may start new traditions. Decorations may be put up again. Different family members or friends may host holiday dinners. Uncles or good friends may replace Dad's spot by taking sons and daughters hunting and fishing or to school events. Special causes or memorials may be set up in their honor—continue to support them indefinitely.

Gwen

Now that the secret is out that grief does not magically disappear after the first year, let's not tell the bereaved. It is not helpful to announce that this pain is a lifetime membership. There is something about the one-year mark that leads us to believe that we have arrived and that the pain will get better. Many times, the first year is a fog, and when the fog lifts, the pain is still present. This is a painful reality that all bereaved people reach, so our job as the helper is to be there in the long haul. To know there is no magical end. To know that no matter how much time has passed, it can seem like forever or just yesterday since the death occurred.

Be intentional. Remembering isn't easy. Create a calendar for important dates, and yes, the date of death is important. Remember to say something, send a card, or make a call. I have met many pastors who, after conducting a funeral service, write on their calendars the contacts they want to make with the bereaved. This is such a good idea. We can get busy with life and forget, which in turn hurts the bereaved. You can take your calendar and every month write the contact you would like to make, based on your geographical and relational closeness to the bereaved. For example, maybe it is to bring a meal once a month or a dessert during a season for the first year or two. Or, it could be a call, text, or note sent. Any acknowledgment is appreciated.

I do believe that honoring the story of the person's life has been a big part of my job; it is easy and can be fun! Sounds crazy, I know, but when I get to hear the story of how they met, what their child was like, the life they lived, it is so beautiful. It is not hard to do but it requires patience, as you may hear the same story several times. Realize that they are not making new memories, so the past is all they have. I have learned so many lessons about life, love, hurt, and healing from hearing their stories that I can say I have the best job in the world. The bereaved do not just want to talk about the death; they want to talk about their living. You too will be changed by the stories you hear. They will add so much to your life, trust me!

The following are two examples that I've experienced during my years as a grief counselor. Both are lessons on how important it is when we intentionally support the bereaved for more than a few weeks after the death.

A pastor and his wife experienced the suicide of their eighteen-year-old daughter. The church was very supportive, giving him a few Sundays off. When I met him, as he presented on a panel of bereaved parents, he shared the most hurtful part of his journey ... the one-year anniversary of his daughter's death was not acknowledged in any way. In fact, it fell on a Sunday, and he had to preach that day. He said, "I wished they thought about how hard that day was for us. Maybe they forgot or were not aware of the date." As a supportive helper, write it down. As you can see, the bereaved are not always aware of when hard days will come, so we need to be proactive and help plan for them, long after the first year.

The second story is about a woman who did not know what to do about her son's Christmas stocking. She thought it would make others uncomfortable if she still hung it on the mantel. When I asked her what *she* wanted, she said, "To me, I still have four children, and I want to hang Steven's stocking with the others." So, I said, "Hang it." We came up with the idea that if anyone said anything negative or judgmental about it, they had to put money in it. Also, the money that would normally go to buy Steven's gift went into the stocking as well. It has been almost twenty years, and friends and family still stuff Steven's stocking with money. His mom buys books for the elementary school he was attending at the time of his death. She places a sticker in the book stating it is given in memory of Steven. This is not only a way for his memory to live on, to creatively make him a part of the holidays, but also for others to acknowledge his life, death, and walk with the family on their lifelong grief journey. Yes, lifelong; that is what I meant when I said long haul. They will not always be actively grieving but they will always remember.

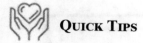 **QUICK TIPS**

- Call/text/email the bereaved no matter how long it's been. It is never too late to remember.
- Remember the bereaved at milestones: (using calendar reminders)
  - Holidays (Mother's Day/Father's Day, Valentine's Day, Memorial Day).
  - Anniversaries (of the death, wedding).
  - Seasons changing, memorable events.
  - The person's birthday.
- Participate/support events that the bereaved have set up in memory of their person.
- Donate to causes in their name and attend memorial functions.
- Invite them to a meal or bring a meal to them, even weeks/months after the loss.

What system can you use to remember important dates? Set your intentions and start now.

_____

_____

_____

_____

_____

_____

CHAPTER TEN

WHAT ABOUT THE KIDS?

· ·

"I have told you these things, so that in me you may have peace. In this world you will have trouble. But take heart! I have overcome the world." (John 16:33)

There is not a person alive who does not experience trouble. We are also instructed to teach our children (Prov. 22:6; Deut. 6;6–7) the ways of the Lord. It is natural to want to focus on the hope and strength we have in Christ and all the good stuff ... yet, there will be troubles. As adults, we do need to be honest with children when hurts arise and to resist the temptation to always try to make things better for them. Begin by acknowledging the trouble, allowing for the pain that comes with it, and, then just like this verse, anchoring in the victory we have in Christ.

· ·

Bethany

Grief is really hard. Add in the responsibility of raising kids or managing a household and it's even harder. Not only did I have to process my own grief, but I had to help my son through his and still be the great mom I wanted to be … and now, try to be the dad, too, for my son and daughter.

I waited a day or two to tell my son that his dad died. There was so much chaos at my house, and he was safe at the neighbor's with people he loved and that I trusted. I was dreading the moment I had to tell my son. I am grateful that when I decided who I wanted to have with me when I told him, none of my family objected or gave me their opinion about it. I didn't hesitate about who I wanted with me: it was Miss Carol.

She wasn't a relative and hadn't been a long-time friend. But I chose her, and she said, "Yes I will." She knew our family, including Kevin, for about a year as part of a county-wide educational program, where she did monthly home visits and taught us about developmental games that we could play with our son. While my ask was not in her job description, she stepped up to support me during my greatest time of need. She probably did not expect to be the one asked to help me in this way, but I am grateful she was willing. Your grieving friend might ask you to help support them in ways you did not expect. Even if it's a little outside of your comfort zone, ask God to help you find the words or help you brave the stillness and support your friend's needs.

In the Resources section at the end of this book, I list several websites and books that I have found helpful in grief support for children. I encourage you to pass along these resources to your friend, or even consider purchasing one of the children's books, with a note of encouragement inside.

A friend of mine worked in a hospice facility at the time Kevin died and was able to provide a DVD to me that helped explain death to children. We didn't watch it right away; it was a few months after Kevin died that I felt it was the right time. Consider reaching out to organizations, explain that you are helping a grieving friend who has children, and ask what resources they might have available that you can pass along.

I decided to put my son into counseling when he started biting around age three, mostly me but sometimes others. (I still feel bad about that, sorry!) I was afraid that the biting was an effect of grief. After several months with a great Christian counselor, it was determined that he was, in fact, very well adjusted to the new normal, and he was acting out via biting as many other normal toddlers do. He outgrew this phase shortly thereafter thank goodness. If you know of a good counselor, either from your experience or from someone else's recommendation, please pass that information on to a grieving parent. You can present it in a helpful way, such as saying you're not sure if they need it or already have someone, but this person was recommended. It can save the grieving person time and money on top of everything else they are going through if they have a personal reference at hand. Present it as a source of support should they need it, not that you are telling them they need to get their child into counseling. There might be situations where that is the case but be gentle while suggesting it.

Grieving people often are overly sensitive, and you don't want to have it be perceived that the grieving person is doing anything wrong or is failing their child. Remember that unless you live with the grieving person and their child(ren), you only see a portion of their behavior. Use caution in making judgments about how they must be reacting to the loss based on the limited views you see. If the child appears to be doing great, it might be true. If they are really struggling and misbehaving, it might be due to the loss or various other factors.

There are many resources on how children are affected by grief, but that is not our focus here. However, I think it's important to understand, as a supportive friend, what I learned that involves the parents and the children. I was told by our counselor that in many cases, depending on the age, children will not fully grieve until they believe their parents are done grieving. Children do not want to see their parents upset or feel like they are the cause for making them upset. They may seem fine because they don't want to add anything else to their parent's plate. What a burden to carry, the delaying of grief for the sake of others. When the surviving parent shows less signs of grief, the child may then show more signs of grief. Think about that: the grieving parent has turned a corner in their grief, but now they see their child struggling more with the death. As you support your friend, it's important to understand these complexities if they are also raising children, and you can continue to check in.

Help with Childcare

When a parent is grieving their loss and they have children at home, it can complicate the grieving process. For me, I was grateful to have my two-year-old son who needed me, and who required my care because I had to keep moving. I had to get up in the morning and get him food, get him ready, and be the best mother I could be for him. I loved the honor of being a full-time, 24/7 mom, however, it was hard. If someone else offered to help with my son so I could concentrate on other tasks I had to get done, I was so grateful. In the months following the loss, I had hours and hours of phone calls and paperwork to get done. It's amazing how many companies and people and agencies you must notify. Then, often you have to follow up and provide "proof," via death certificate, to go along with the process. Knowing that someone else was caring for my son so I could get this paperwork done was a Godsend. Offer to provide childcare, if you can. Make sure the grieving person is comfortable with you doing so, especially if it is in their home. Maybe there is a basement or backyard you could offer to play with the child for an hour or more so they can get some things done. It may not seem like much, but it is a huge help.

I had a neighbor, also a trusted family friend, who offered to watch my son for me multiple times. She had been told by other family members that I used to do my grocery shopping at night, after my son went to bed and my husband listened out for him. After my husband died, one of my million thoughts was, *when am I going to be able to grocery shop?* This neighbor realized a need and was specific with her offer. She stopped by several times, and said, "I know you like to go grocery shopping in the evening, and I'd be glad to come over and listen for your son in case he wakes up." Not only did she offer this, but she meant it. She offered several times before I took her up on it. It was hard for me to accept help, but the consistent, genuine offers finally got through to me. (Hint, hint! To repeat: consistent and genuine offers, multiple times.) This special friend, Bonita, even said that it would be a blessing to her if I could allow her to help in this way; that really made me think. The tables seemed to turn and instead of me asking for help or accepting help, I was helping her to feel blessed. It sounds strange but it worked. It made me feel less needy and more at peace with the offers of help. Consider phrasing your offers of help in this way.

A different neighbor, whom I didn't know super well but was friendly to me, stopped by one day and asked if I wanted to join her in taking a Zumba class. What a great and kind offer. Being a grieving person is so hard mentally and physically, and exercise is always very important, especially when grieving. I was hesitant initially, thinking of the childcare dilemma. I immediately thought of the kind neighbor, who had offered help so many times before. By then, I felt comfortable reaching out and asking if she would watch him once a week for eight weeks so I could take this class. She said yes, and I was so grateful. Years after my second tragedy, she would offer to watch my daughter part-time for several months, so that I could complete an internship for my master's degree. My mom also shared in this childcare, traveling from two hours away. I could not have made this internship work without them.

Another time, I was looking into joining a small group at church but the childcare dilemma, as always, existed. When a neighbor friend heard this desire, her teenage son offered to hang out with my son every other week for the entire school year so that I could attend this group. His parents relayed that he wanted to do this completely free of charge. He told them, which they relayed to me, "What else are neighbors for, if not to be helpful?" What a blessing this was. I know your time is precious and limited, however, by you being willing to give of your time, it is so helpful.

Years after my second loss, I was adjusting to hectic kids schedules and I was feeling overwhelmed. I wasn't "grieving," at this point but life was hard. While I was venting my frustrations to a group of friends one of them offered to take my son to his weekly piano lesson so that I could get my daughter to bed earlier. It was a specific offer and I jumped at it mostly because of the way she phrased it. She said, "Can I do this for you" instead of "if you need help" or "if you need me to." Those latter statements tend to prompt an automatic, "no, I can do it" response because on the inside they feel they "must" do it on their own.

If you offer to help provide care for a child, be specific, genuine, and consistent. They might say they'll think about it or politely decline, but don't hesitate to ask again. It's not easy to leave your children in the care of another, but if they trust you, know that you are helping them in a major way. No matter if the grieving person wants to get their nails done, go for a walk, grocery shop, take a class, sleep, etc., try not to put conditions on when you'll watch their children or judge the reason that the grieving person needs childcare in the first place. Make it clear that you're glad to help them however they need help.

I am not suggesting you have no boundaries, though. There could be cases where your offer goes beyond what you are comfortable with, and it's ok to say so. For example, you aren't offering to become their new childcare full time or consistent provider per se, unless you blatantly say you are.

Helping to Fill the Gap

Another way in which you can help a grieving person with their children is to think of what that child might be missing and try to help fill the gap. Because my son lost his father at such a young age, I've relied on grandpas, uncles, and neighbors to take my son golfing, fix things around the house, assemble furniture, and teach him how to mow the yard. One of the most valuable offers I accepted was from my husband's cousin, who took my son every week to his Cub Scout meeting. To me, that meant the world that he would give up so much time and effort to be a father figure to my son. Not only that, but this cousin and two of his sons also took turns attending scout camps with my son over the course of several years. It made my son feel included and special, since other kids had dads attending. He has continued with scouts, and even earned his Eagle rank, but he might not have if we didn't have such great support from them and several key scout parents and leaders.

Another neighbor would often toss the football around with my son when we were outside. To some, this may not seem like a big deal, but it is. That neighbor took my son to his first college football game, too. Even though the game was for my college rival team, I was so thankful he was offered this opportunity with a trusted neighbor and a great role model. I can't overstate how much it means to single parents, especially in situations like mine where the other parent is gone. To know that there are trusted friends or family that are willing to fill that gap, even if it's for an hour occasionally, is very special and helpful. When you step up to be a volunteer for a sports team, a club, a troop, or a league, know that your impact may be farther reaching than you might have thought. Not only are you spending time with your child, but you may also be filling that gap for a child whose parent cannot be involved. It is so appreciated. When my son played in a basketball league, I can clearly recall a moment when my eyes filled with tears of joy and pride when he made his first basket. It was not only the fact that he contributed to his team's score but also the reactions from coaches. They were cheering and clapping and encouraging him. It was a moment filled with very mixed emotions since my husband, his dad, was not there. These dads were the closest thing we had at that moment to a proud dad. Know that you aren't just a "coach," but you're helping to fill the gap.

The wife of the cousin who took my son to Scouts, often attended doctor's visits with me when I was pregnant with my daughter and was by my side in the delivery room when she was born. Talk about a family that has stepped in to fill the gaps! They had a great love and respect for Kevin and continued that love for me and my kids. Obviously, this was a very personal experience but offering to accompany single moms to appointments is also a great way to help.

Encourage Kids to Be Kids

Please don't put added pressure on kids to grow up faster than they already are. I know at least a few people told my son that he was the "man of the house," but this is so cliché and unfair. What does that even mean? That a child now needs to be an authority figure in the house? That they now must take on adult responsibilities? Even if it is said in a light-hearted way, it doesn't sit well with most grieving people. The grieving person still wants their child to be a child, to have as normal of a life as possible despite this huge loss. It's fine to offer to be available to help teach kids skills along the way that their deceased parent would have taught them—that is respectable and awesome but at the age-appropriate time.

Step Up and Offer to Step In

Include, invite, offer to teach something that a deceased parent would have done. Teach the child about their parent since they can no longer know first-hand.

A great friend of Kevin's recently took my son out to dinner and shared stories of his and my husband's times together. They were hunting and fishing buddies and just overall best friends. He knew my husband before I did and has stories I wasn't a part of and didn't know. My son loved hearing more about his dad, especially as he is getting older and more curious about his dad's likes and dislikes, and knowing who he really was from a different perspective. That same friend is now teaching my son how to do oil changes in our cars, something he would have learned from his dad. The friend is helping my son and me.

If you had a relationship with someone who died, consider writing down stories, funny experiences, or what you most admired about that person who has now died. Memories fade and you may not remember the stories forever, so write them down now and share them with your late friend's kids. If you find pictures, provide those, too. It's so easy now to email photos without having to get copies officially made. I have had pictures of my husband sent to me over the years by various family members; I'm so grateful to share them with my son now.

I mentioned above that when you volunteer for your child's group/league/troop, you are not only helping your child but potentially other children who don't have a parent who is able to volunteer. What if you don't have a child in a club, but you still have time or the will to give? Consider volunteering in a scout troop that the grieving person's child is a part of, or be a mentor or tutor for them, or show up to their sports practices or games. Showing up to cheer them on is a big help, believe me!

Results from a 2017 New York Life Foundation survey confirmed that even small gestures helped kids who were coping with the death of a parent. Not only making the effort after the death happens but continuing beyond the first few months of the loss. About 57 percent of Millennials and GenXers who experienced the death of a parent before the age of twenty indicated that their support dropped off heavily after three months. Another result of the survey indicated that it took nearly six years or more to be able to move forward after the death of a parent.[34] That means for us, those that are caring for and about grieving children, need to keep the support and care going for much longer.

Most of this chapter has been about a child who has suffered a loss due to death. Children whose parents get divorced or when a parent is incarcerated or separated from the family, or if a parent or sibling is diagnosed with a serious medical illness, are also affected by grief. Keep in mind these situations are all complicated, but if your heart is in the right place and you want to help with the children, make sure to talk to the parent(s) about your offer of help first and get their permission. Typically, if a child is diagnosed with a serious illness, they are the focus of support. But if there are other siblings at home, they can often be forgotten. Depending on their age, they understand the support would be with the sick child. However, the healthy child is going through a tremendously hard time, too. They are worried about their family member, but their world has changed as well. Mom and Dad are not home as much

---

[34] "New Survey on Childhood Grief Reveals Substantial 'Grief Gap,'" New York Life Foundation, November 15, 2017, https://www.newyorklife.com/newsroom/2017/parental-loss-survey.

because they are caring for the sick child, for example. Holiday traditions may change, and vacations may be limited right now. They may experience major shifts in family dynamics and see their parents upset and stressed more than ever. The siblings need care, too. What has helped these siblings is people acknowledging their grief and hard times—even a note sent to them or a text, "thinking of you." Don't assume that they can't attend events or don't want to laugh because their family member is ill—they still need and want to have a "normal" life.

In the case of divorce or incarceration, please be sure that you never bad-mouth either parent or give any information about the situation that you might know to the unknowing child. Realize that it is the parent(s) job to handle explaining to their children in their own way. Do not give any information to the child about the personal situation or assume that they know all the facts. In my second tragic situation, my son was grieving the loss of my second husband, his stepdad, and his sudden incarceration. He had grown close to him and was grieving the loss of "another" dad. I'm so grateful that no one gave any information to my son that I didn't feel he was ready to hear and understood that he was sad about his stepdad being suddenly gone, even though everyone knew it was the right thing to happen in his case.

I once read that a high percentage of prison inmates on death row experienced the death of a parent at a young age. An even higher percentage of incarcerated teens had a significant person in their life that had died. That really got me thinking. *Did these individuals have people that stepped in and guided them, mentored them, and tried to fill the role of the missing parent?* Of course, there are so many variables, but it makes me realize the long-lasting and serious impact that a parental death can have on children. Similarly, the death of their sibling or any other family member or friend that they were close to may adversely affect them for the rest of their lives if they don't get the right support. It's important to understand this and learn where we can do better and step in.

Thank you for considering the additional stress that grieving people are under when they are also raising children that are affected by grief. Parenting is hard enough, let alone when the parents and children are both grieving. There are ways to help, and I'm grateful for those that do.

Gwen

When Billy Crystal was asked by Barbara Walters what his father's death did to him, his response seemed to rock the always steady and assured interviewer. He said, "It's also *still* doing to me."[35] Billy was just fifteen when his father died. We know that children, like adults, can have meaningful lives after experiencing devastating losses, but Billy's response reminds us that it will always be a part of our lives.

By gaining a basic understanding of children's grief, you'll be better able to help your grieving friend and what they are facing. Dr. Sandra Fox points out "Four Tasks of Children's Grief," and I've given a few tips under each task. Just remember that the parents take the lead and have the final say on how information and feelings are handled in their family.

---

[35] Billy Crystal, "Barbara Walters Special: Robin Williams, Billy Crystal, and Jay Leno: September 26, 1989," interview by Barbara Walters, *The Barbara Walters Special*, ABC, September 26, 1989, 12:40, https://www.youtube.com/watch?v=oyh6Jl0WoDY.

Dr. Sandra Fox explained the Four Tasks of Children's Grief:[36]

1. Understanding: Knowing the loss really happened and is real.

Clear and simple explanations are best. Avoid religious responses such as "God needed an extra angel, so He took your sister." One repercussion of this could lead the surviving child to not want to behave *too* well for fear God will take them also. They can understand that the body stopped working. They can even understand some diagnoses, but oftentimes, we talk around what happened, and the children are left confused.

Thank God children do not have the same grieving mode we do as adults. They bounce back much quicker, wanting to play and have fun between their emotional responses. It is hard to remember that as adults, our hearts are breaking for the kids, but they are not processing in the same way we do.

2. Grieving: Working through the various feelings that are a part of mourning.

Mister Rogers' Neighborhood Fred Rogers said, "Anything that's human is mentionable, and anything that's mentionable can be more manageable... When we can talk about our feelings, they can become less overwhelming, less upsetting, and less scary."[37]

Providing other trusting adults for children to have a safe place to "dump" their feelings, since we know, they do not want to add to the surviving parents' pain, is a good idea. You, the reader, do not

---

[36] Sandra Sutherland Fox, *Good Grief: Helping Groups of Children When a Friend Dies* (Boston: New England Association for the Education of Young Children, 1985), XX.

[37] Fred Rogers, *A Beautiful Day in the Neighborhood: Neighborly Words of Wisdom from Mister Rogers* (New York: Penguin Books, 2019), 111.

have to be that person, but if you can make sure there are people in that role, it is very helpful. Being good role models for healthy expression of feelings is very valuable as well. We do not need to share all our pain with children, but it is healthy for them to see us sad and expressing our feelings, rather than hiding them.

3. **Commemorating: Some way of remembering, observing, or memorializing the loss. Provides an opportunity for affirming the value or the life of the person—or other types of loss.**

Talking about those who have died gives value to the lives left behind. If we no longer talk about Grandpa, then children sub-consciously draw the conclusion that if they die, it won't matter because no one would talk or remember them either. The capturing of stories about their person is important. We also need to cap-ture what their hearts recall and remember, too. Memory work is so helpful, such as pillows painted with fabric markers, memory books/boxes, collages, drawings, etc. You do not have to be the person to do it with them, but consider sharing these ideas with your friend and help make sure it happens if they are in agreement. There are so many wonderful grief camps and groups that children can go to, where memory work is a big part of their healing. It allows them, years later, to see what their little minds remember about their person. See resources in the back of the book to find a support center or camp for children, and consider contributing funds for these camps if that is a need your friend has.

4. Going on: Permission is needed from significant others that it is OK to get on with life and OK to "re-grieve" should the feelings return.

The fourth task of children's grief is *moving on*. Children do not want to stay in "grief mode" too long. They need permission to have fun and be involved in life; grief takes a lifetime, but they don't have to stay in the well of sorrow forever. It does get better, and life goes on. Often children learn compassion and empathy, and the change this brought in their lives can have some positives as well. As friends, you can invite the grieving children/family to join you in activities. I am reminded of two elementary school children whose father died the day before Valentine's Day. They wanted to go to school so as not to miss the party. Although this was too much for their mother, her friends were able to help get the children to school with all their Valentine's cards/treats. Routine is good for children and as friends, we can help maintain that for them by offering to do the day-to-day, and sometimes extra special events for them.

Let's face it; without loss, child-rearing is not an easy task. It takes a team. In dancing, we keep to the beat of the music. Even in the best rhythms of life, childhood and adolescence are hard. Sometimes they want/need adults close; sometimes they don't. We are often left trying to figure out what they want. Even now, with all this information, you may be at a loss of how to help with the kids, so ask. Their life is out of rhythm, and it will change many times as they learn what it looks like now. Be flexible; see where you may be able to step in and take a few laps around to help support them.

 **QUICK TIPS**

- Offer to watch a grieving person's children—be intentional and consistent and clear.
- Offer to fill in the gap where the deceased person would have participated.
- Offer several times, if needed, but refrain from being pushy.
- Don't be too concerned, nosey, or judgmental with the reason that the grieving person needs help with childcare; it could be to take care of business regarding the death, but it could be so they can take a nap. It's equally helpful.
- Provide resources for the grieving person (books, counselors), but understand it is their decision to pursue it or not and on their time frame.
- Write a letter about the deceased person so that the grieving person can give it to their children when they are ready for it—include stories and other traits that you liked about that person.
- Understand that a grieving person has extra burdens and layers of grief if they are also caring for children; give them extra grace.
- Ask the parent(s) for permission with any ideas you have in helping with the children.

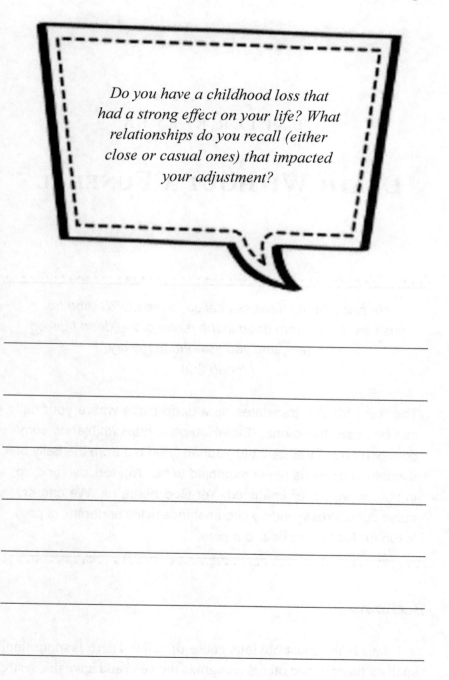

Do you have a childhood loss that had a strong effect on your life? What relationships do you recall (either close or casual ones) that impacted your adjustment?

_____

_____

_____

_____

_____

_____

CHAPTER ELEVEN

DEATH WITHOUT A FUNERAL

• •

He said: "In my distress I called to the LORD, and he answered me. From deep in the realm of the dead I called for help, and you listened to my cry."
(Jonah 2:2)

The word "depth" translates as a deep place where your call can be heard by no one. (BibleHub.com, https://biblehub.com/commentaries/jonah/2-2.htm) Jonah cried out from the belly of a whale, a place he never expected to be. We, too, can end up in places we never imagined. Yet God hears us. We can cry out in our distress, and no circumstance in life or depths of pain is too far for God to hear our plea.

• •

Bethany

Death is the most obvious cause of grief. There is mourning, usually a funeral, and others recognize the need and have the desire to support. There are defined event dates: the day of death, the viewing/funeral, and other typical and expected hard days. At any given time, we all know someone who has recently experienced the death of someone close to them. However, unless you work in a hospital, nursing home, funeral home, as a first responder, or on a battlefield, it's not likely that you are experiencing death daily. What we experience more commonly is people who are struggling, or have struggled, with a figurative death. These are not always visible but can still be very hard on the person experiencing it. I won't say a figurative death is "as bad" as a literal death; in some cases, it could be worse. It's very dangerous to make comparisons, as each loss is complicated, and the extent to which a person grieves varies based on so many factors. While a figurative death isn't a physical death of a body, it is the death or destruction of some "thing." This usually is the death of a dream, of plans, of a future that is not going to happen now in the way that we thought.

When I experienced my second tragedy, I quickly realized I was in "grief mode" again. While my ex-husband hadn't died, the story of "us" died. Many dreams, plans, and our future together died. My ability to trust another man essentially died (still hoping one day to get that back but as of press date, it hasn't happened). Again, my support system circled around me and helped me through, but I realized there were other people experiencing divorce and losses that weren't as well cared for. Take it from me after experiencing both types of "death"; supportive care is critical in healing from all types of losses.

Examples of figurative deaths that I'll explore here are due to divorce (or end of a serious relationship), job loss, incarceration, and medical diagnosis. There could be, and likely are, others. Any loss that a person feels that causes them to grieve is their own real pain, whether or not others feel it is a "justified" loss or not.

Divorce

When I was growing up in the 1980s, divorce seemed rare, and I cannot even think of a childhood friend whose parents were divorced. Now, we all likely know several couples that have gone through a divorce. Some may have been a very surprising result, and others maybe not as much. The statistics on divorce are complicated, with some states not reporting their data, couples waiting longer to get married, and divorce rates varying between age groups. General beliefs are that up to 50 percent of marriages end in divorce, and in each subsequent marriage, the percentage is higher. I could spend hours interpreting charts to tell you what you already know: divorce happens, and it can result in grief—for the two involved plus any children, grandparents, friends, and more. For this topic, I will use the word "divorce," but keep in mind there are some long-term couples that don't technically "marry" but suffer grief if they go through a separation as well.

What are the first two words that come to your mind when you hear that someone got divorced? Most people would think, *what happened?* Thanks to human curiosity, we want to know what the reason is. Who did what? Did someone cheat? We hope there is a "justifiable" reason, which I believe is a natural desire for humans to want to see things whole. When something breaks, we try to figure out why it broke and hope that it doesn't happen to us. Maybe you have insight into why the couple got divorced, and you might be able to speculate with a degree of certainty what the reason is. No matter what insight you may have, please keep it to yourself. Avoid the temptation to be the source of information. A wise friend once told me she would keep something I told her confidential because she said, "It's not my story to tell." It's not your story to tell; it's an opportunity to let your heart care for and support a person in need, and that should be the focus.

Divorced people often face judgment from others. They may be facing financial struggles, high stress, big decisions, and grief. Even if divorce is the best solution for them, it is still a difficult decision. When a couple gets divorced, we often think of the details first (how/why did this happen) and base our sympathy on the reasons we find out or speculate. If we hear the husband cheated, then we don't tend to feel as bad for him, right? If we hear the wife was spending all his money, we feel less bad for her and hope she gets her priorities straight. If we have no idea what happened, we look for signs or hope to find out the details at some point. And/or, we may keep our distance because we want to give them privacy. I think there is a clear absence of care for divorced people. We focus on the "whys" and not the "needs." We tend to be more "hands off," since both people are still alive and handling the issues between the two of them.

There's a negative connotation for a "divorced" person as compared to a widow, no doubt about it. There are also added complications when a couple gets divorced in the public eye, if they were both active in church or attended the same church, if there are children involved, or if they work at the same place. For Christians in particular, we need to make sure we are still welcoming and caring for all people. Remember that you don't and won't truly know what happened between two divorced people—only the two of them know. Justifiable divorce is not yours to decide, but whether or not you care for those hurting is your decision.

Divorce can cause people to suffer from damaged self-esteem. Depending on the factors of the divorce, it can leave either partner to question if there is something wrong with them which caused the break in the bond. This can lead to depression and anxiety mixed with the confusion and sadness of grief. Do your best as a caring friend to lift them up, make them feel loved and lovable, cared for and to know that they are still valuable and important. Let them know you don't expect to hear details about the loss; you just want to be there for them. This reassures the divorced person that you aren't there for the wrong reasons, and they may be able to accept support a little better. In what areas of their life can you offer support? Meals, childcare, friendship: some of the ways previously discussed for grieving people you can consider for people going through a divorce.

Job Loss

Pretty much gone are the days where an employee stays with a company for their entire career. It happens, but it is becoming more and more rare. There is less loyalty to a company and more loyalty to professional growth, along with generally getting more comfortable with change. This can be an increase in pay, a change of direction, or better opportunities. Companies are constantly needing to adjust to stay viable and competitive in the marketplace. As such, employees can find themselves displaced due to no real fault of their own—downsizing, reorganizing, or reduction in force. In the year 2020, many employees found themselves displaced due to the coronavirus pandemic, which forced many companies to shut down for a period of time or even for good, laying off or losing many of their employees. There are also cases of employees losing their jobs perhaps due to a partial or full fault of their own—performance or policy violations, or not seeing eye to eye with a decision-maker at their company. Whatever the reason, these employees who are displaced can be thrown into grieving. This could be related to the loss of dreams, of stability, of plans, and fear of the unknown.

As with the case of divorce, some people like to speculate why a person lost their job. Unless you are a trusted friend, you might never hear the full story, but does it really matter? If you care about this person, think of their needs and how you can help. Realize that they are likely searching for another job and may be physically and mentally drained from the stress. This may be a blow to their self-esteem, similar to a divorce situation. It may be overwhelming to think about the need to search for a job, create a résumé for the first time in decades, go through exhausting interviews, potentially compete with more qualified candidates, and maybe face the requirement to learn new skills. The thought of losing friendships with coworkers can be sad. The pressure of needing to find a replacement income sooner rather than later can add to the stress they are feeling. The responsibility that breadwinners have can be daunting when it's uncertain, and change is always hard, even if it ends up being a positive one eventually.

Jay experienced grief not only from the death of his parents and brother, but also from job loss.[38] After having been with a company for over two decades, he was stunned to find out his job was being eliminated. He continued to work in that role for about four months, while at the same time trying to find another role within the company. There was a lot of fear, but he had a positive and professional attitude. What was most helpful during that time was friends and coworkers continuing to check in on him. His pastor reached out several times and complimented him on his way of handling this news with grace. Though he seemed to handle the situation well, Jay still was comforted by the care of others and intentional reach-outs. He appreciated the notes, texts, and emails of people who were specific and genuine in their desire to wish him well, that they were thinking of him, and offered to listen if he needed to talk. Jay points out that with most men it takes a few nudges to get them to open up. It might take a few offers of help before it's accepted. It might take a few "How are you? No, how are you *really* doing" offers before he would answer honestly. He advises, "Still offer help even if you think they won't take it.

---

[38] Personal interview with the author, November 22, 2022, Used with permission.

They might take it, they might not, but they very much appreciate the offer." Simple, heartfelt sentiments like, "Sorry you are going through this," were meaningful. What wasn't helpful is when people bashed the company and almost pushed him deeper into a pit of despair. These people might have felt that they were expressing their frustration on behalf of their friend, but it wasn't always helpful. Some instances of sharing similar bad experiences that the company has caused them or agreeing that "this situation totally sucks" can be bonding, but don't overdo it. Don't leave the person with just that—it could make them feel worse.

Consider how adding some hope or encouragement is helpful. Amid his job searching, Jay was supposed to go on a guys' trip to Colorado with friends. With an uncertain future, he considered canceling his trip. His supportive wife encouraged him to go even with financial uncertainty because she knew he needed a break from the stress. During that trip, one of the guys confided that he, too, had several situations of job displacement that Jay didn't realize had happened. It was such a relief, really, to know that he was not alone, that others had made it through similar situations, and there was hope. He was glad his friend shared his experience in a way that gave him a different perspective.

What is the best way to help someone who has lost their job? Reach out to them, let them know you are thinking of them, and offer what you can. Let them know specifically what you have to offer, based on what your gifts are—maybe it's a network of contacts in the field that they are seeking. Maybe it's to watch the kids while they go on interviews. Maybe it is offering to look over their résumé and provide suggestions for refining it. Maybe it is just an invitation to coffee and help them find a change of pace from job searching. Whatever your offer is, make it genuine and non-judgmental. Don't put yourself in a position of offering to help when you really don't intend to. Be prepared to follow up on offers and nudge them a couple of times if they don't accept help right away.

And that "help" may just be checking in on them, offering to meet for lunch or a drink, and just being there with them. Remember that the stress and uncertainty aren't just about their nine to five job. It is fear of how the future will shape up now with this lapse in employment, taking care of everyday needs, and the effects being home has on other members of the family and their normal routine.

Their grief might not last as long if they are able to find another job, but there are so many variables that it's best to be kind and supportive regardless—and change is hard. Even if they find a new job, it may be very different from what they were used to; it might not be what they want to be doing, and they may have made changes to make the new job work. It's never too late to check in and just let them know you're thinking of them.

Incarceration of a Family Member

In my second tragedy, I was newly married to a husband who had now been arrested for horrible crimes and was facing a long prison sentence. Because of the awfulness of the crimes, there was a lot of shame I felt, even though I had no idea of what had been going on in the short seven weeks that we had been married, or for any time before that. While I knew for certain his incarceration was justified, it was still incredibly sad that my marriage to who I thought he was had died. I had never experienced anyone close to me being incarcerated, so it was all new territory for me. There were so many details (personal and logistical) that I needed to sort out with him. I visited him in jail several times, trying to get answers both to understand what had happened and practical answers such as where to find this key, or that document. I needed to talk to him to fully process what was happening. It was awful. While I sat and waited for my "turn" to talk to him through a plexi-glass wall, I prayed for all the people in the waiting room. There was a common, melancholy attitude that this was not where they wanted to be. Whether it is your first or fiftieth time visiting there, it is a stressful, awkward, and surreal situation. One never wants this to be their reality. The loss of control in the situation, the limits you have on when and for how long you can talk to the incarcerated person, and the loss of privacy is obvious at jail visitations.

How did people support me regarding this incarceration? I had a cousin drive me to see my ex-husband for the first time. I had no idea what to expect, and she helped me not experience it alone. She sat next to me in the waiting room and helped fill the awkward silence and calm my nerves. She didn't judge me for wanting to go; she didn't pry after I talked to him. She just cared for me. Another friend listened to me when I would call her after my visits. She didn't ask for details, but I felt comfortable telling her how the visit went and how I was feeling. When I visited him for what I felt would be the last time, I called her as usual. When I relayed that I felt this was the last visit, she sighed and said that she was glad to hear that. She explained that she never judged me for going but was relieved to hear that I wouldn't be putting myself through it any longer. My friend went on to say that she knew I had to decide on my own to be "done" and that because she wasn't in my shoes, she didn't feel she could tell me not to go. (Did I mention I have wonderful friends?) She cared for me, worried about me but respected my decisions.

For the parents of an incarcerated child, they are facing grief as well, especially if the sentence is long-term. They may wonder where they went wrong in raising their child or feel that others are judging them as parents. They may fear that their child's choices are a reflection of them as people, and "why" is a common question they ask themselves. This work of sorting through where this child went wrong takes a lot of prayer, patience, and sometimes a lot of counseling. These parents deserve our care and compassion, without judgement. There are so many variables in situations of incarceration, it's best to support the affected grieving people and not engage in speculation. Parents may disagree that their child is incarcerated, or they may accept that jail/prison is the appropriate place for their child given the circumstances. Either way, it is an incredibly hard situation and if your friend is in this situation, they need your support.

Parents of incarcerated people face not only the death of their child's dreams and plans but of their own as well. It's not to say that an incarcerated person's life is over; they still have opportunities to heal, learn from their mistakes, and learn to be a better person. It's possible once released, if able to be released, they will begin a new life on a better path. For others that have life sentences, they have a choice to make the best of their surroundings—God is not done with them yet. They can make a difference within their walls to still use their God-given gifts in a manner different than anyone might have previously dreamed.

Author Carol Kent tells an impactful story of her son, Jason, who was sentenced to life in prison in Florida for one horribly bad decision. He was their only child, and they faced deep grief when they realized that their dreams for him may never flourish. The stress and publicity of the situation, sorting out facts, the shock of trying to understand how their caring and protective son could commit such a crime. The bright light that came out of the tragedy with their son is a ministry they started called "Speak Up for Hope," which offers hope and healing to inmates and their families. With support from around the world, Carol and her husband, Gene, are able to support other inmates with basic needs and care for visitors who are waiting to visit their incarcerated relatives. They don't judge why the incarcerations happened, but rather focus on how they can help and serve those who are grieving. One way in which Carol and Gene have been supported is by people who have supported their ministry and sent their son a birthday card in prison. They talk about how much it uplifts his spirit and, in turn, theirs.[39] They also collect donations of black T-shirts, which they hand out to visitors to the jail that didn't otherwise meet the "acceptable apparel" for visiting inmates. People who drove for hours to visit but would be turned away since they were wearing a sleeveless shirt, for example, could be given one of these donated T-shirts and still be able to visit their inmate. By contributing to a ministry such as this, you are blessing Carol and Gene's desire to help grieving family members be able to visit without worry of a clothing technicality.

Think, also, of children whose parents are incarcerated. There are many factors that may affect the children's feelings (how long the incarcerated parent will be absent, how old the child was at the time of incarceration, and the reason, among other factors). Children who feel this intense loss with the separation of their parent/relative are grieving the absence and are often scared about the unknown of their current situation. They may feel ashamed, isolated and might withdraw from their friends and activities. How we treat the children in these cases is critical. It can be awkward when talking generally about "dads" or "moms" or "grandparents" when theirs is absent. It's so valuable to offer to step in (with permission of course) where the child might be missing that parental figure, just as you would for a child enduring a death.

Medical Diagnosis Grief

When each of my children were born, I prayed for two things: that they would be healthy and happy. Like many parents, my prayers were answered upon their birth and to this day. But for many others, they have faced the news or gotten the call that their loved one is not healthy and is facing a scary road ahead. This

---

[39] Carol Kent, "Our Story," Speak Up for Hope, https://speakupforhope.org/our-story.

could be in the form of birth defects, childhood cancer, any sort of diagnosis that is going to make their road a little (or a lot) tougher. Many people each day get "the call" or find out the news that their check-up, rash, bump, or symptoms are connected to a much bigger problem. Their world has now shifted in focus. Maybe they need to take a leave from their jobs, quit, or endure months of doctor appointments or intensive treatments, surgeries, therapies, or medicine. The span of possibilities here is too numerous to explore, but we can likely all think of a family who has received the news that their family member is not okay. What was planned and what the future held might be different from here on out. It might be a temporary condition or a life-long and life-altering adjustment. There may be a feeling of a figurative "death" of how you thought plans were going to be for this person, and the road ahead can often feel lonely.

When my friend Laura's son was diagnosed with a cancerous brain tumor, he had surgeries and multiple treatments for more than a year.[40] The support was mostly overwhelmingly awesome. In the beginning of this journey, the hospital social worker warned her that typically the support would drop off or stop, but Laura did not believe that would be the case. However, she discovered that it's hard for people to keep supporting for the long haul. She understood why, because she, too, had found herself not checking up on people in her life as much or for as long as she would like to. Once you experience the fading of support or learn about how sad it can be to experience, you try to do better. She mentioned that incredibly there are people who are very intentional with text messages or consistent with cards. There was a woman who faithfully sent a card to her son with a joke and encouraging words. Apparently, this woman knew someone who worked for Laura's husband and

---

[40] Personal Communication with author, December 3, 2022. Used with permission.

had heard about her son's illness, though Laura had never met this thoughtful woman.

The cards started out once a week and changed to once a month, but a year in, they continued. Laura also created a Facebook care page so that people who wanted updates could get them in one place, and so she didn't have to keep track of who she was telling what to (another stressor). Laura's wish was to: stay with me. We have good days, but we still have bad days. She also wanted to still be included on other's prayer requests, too. She started joining friends on occasional dinners out and a short get-away, which restored her. Yes, she was tired and busy, but still feeling included was so important to her.

Gwen

> "Life is made up of sobs, sniffles, and smiles, with sniffles predominating."—O. Henry[41]

In other words, life has its ups and downs.

That is not news to you. There are many things, other than death, that cause great pain. Somehow, we do not recognize their difficulty and again, we stand in judgment of how they "should" be handled. It can be due to our need to keep life full of smiles, to want to ride the ups with people but to deny or ignore the downs. Acknowledgment is key. Recognize that there is both pain and need when someone you know is experiencing the following losses.

Job loss: This can attack our self-confidence greatly. Listening and support are good and needed, but connections are important. Ask others in your circle if they know of jobs, and then give that information to the job seeker. Allow for spaces of tougher conversations

---

[41] O. Henry, "The Gifts of the Magi," *New York Sunday World*, December 10, 1905, https://americanliterature.com/author/o-henry/short-story/the-gift-of-the-magi.

as to other needs, such as food, help with their bills, or other areas. You don't have to pry for details; you can simply say, "If you have needs, I would like to help you connect to resources, and we can do this as confidentially as possible." Our church hosted a mobile food pantry, one of the regular workers recently experienced job loss so I very discreetly whispered to her, "I would like to put a box of food in your van; just nod and it will be done and no one else will know." I knew her pride would not allow her to go from being the "helper" of those in need to be "the" needy. We have never talked about it but as long as she didn't have a job, I put a box in her van every time.

Divorce: I read grief books frequently due to my profession, so when I was asked by my pastor to lead a divorce workshop at our church, I started to read about divorce. I needed to research, especially since I am not divorced and, at that time, had very little exposure to it. I was on an airplane reading a book with a title that clearly indicated it was a self-help resource for people going through a divorce. I did not realize until that time in the airport, and on the plane, that most people do not read a book like that openly in public. The reactions and comments I received while holding this book were very interesting. I felt many "I'm sorry" looks. I also was gently patted on my shoulder as they passed me. More than anything, complete strangers spilled their tea with, "Let me tell you about my divorce." Those conversations taught me more than the book.

Death, including suicide, is viewed as an event we couldn't control. Death is a part of every life, but divorce is not part of every marriage, and we certainly do not enter it thinking it is going to happen to us. It seems divorce leaves behind more questions, unfinished business, hurt, anger, and disappointment than death loss. There is no formalized ceremony when your marriage dies. No one brings you lasagna; people do not wait in line to offer sympathy or support at the casket of your dead marriage. A deceased spouse does not come to get the kids every other weekend, nor do you have to face them moving on or remarrying. There are differences, but there are commonalities as well. Keep this in mind when considering your divorced friends, not just friends that lose a spouse due to death.

When my sister, who is divorced, had her first date with a widowed man, she called me and asked what she needed to know about widowers. I let her know that his wife will always have a place in his heart, his home, and certainly with his children. They would likely still be married had death not so rudely interrupted their life together. In explaining further, I said, "You do not have pictures of your ex-husband on the walls of your home, but I am sure he has pictures of her on his walls." She went on to not only date him but married him in 2009, and he is still my brother-in-law today. His first wife, Kathy, is someone who my children know through stories, and there are pictures of her in his home office. She continues to have a place. Many divorced couples do have healthy relationships after their marriage ends, which is so awesome for the children. It is up to us to follow the lead on where the ex fits now, but we cannot force a continued relationship.

Divorce can be an area where curious people want to know the "dirt." I suggest coming up with a uniform reply that is shared with the general population, those outside your inner circle (and yes, the family can be outside the inner circle). When my sister divorced, she decided to use a created standard response for those continual inquiries. The statement was: "After countless prayers and years of counseling, we are sorry to say this marriage cannot be saved." This lets people know that Jesus was consulted, they did try to save it, and they are very sad. That is all people need to know. I have had many people borrow this since. If your friends need a statement, feel free to offer it. As her sister, I received many phone calls from people just wanting to know "What happened to her marriage?"

They got the uniform reply, no matter how many times they asked. If you, too, are on the receiving end of a general statement, do not be offended. Respect that this is all that they want shared for now.

Medical diagnosis: Whether your friend is losing their person a bit at a time due to a physical or mental deterioration or your friend is losing himself, it is necessary to mourn. With many illnesses, a loss occurs every day, as they no longer have the function they had yesterday. As we watch a person in pain, not being able to do all they used to do, it is so hard on family and friends, but it is also hard for the person. I have reminded well-meaning family and friends who want to spend lengthy time (emotionally charged, I might add) seeing the ill before they die, that they have just this one goodbye to say, but the dying person has many goodbyes. Therefore, the patient may choose not to have emotional goodbyes with everyone—it is too much. So don't be offended when visits are declined, or you are not included in some things. If you are invited, keep it short. They are tired. Overstaying your welcome is a sure way to not be invited back or to create more stress and anguish. Allow the patient/ill person to lead: you can ask, "Do you feel like talking today?" Or "Is there anything that you may need help with?" If they say no, move on.

As my dad was in hospice care for nine months, laying in a hospital bed with end-stage Parkinson's disease, I would often ask if there was anything he wanted to talk about. I asked if he was worried about anything or needed help with anything, but he always answered no. I asked; he answered; I moved on. Did I want to know all his inner thoughts, struggles, and concerns? Of course. Wasn't I the perfect person for him to talk to about these things since I do this with so many others? Yes, I thought so. But he said no. Just to ease my heart, I did have the hospice chaplain ask him too, and he got the same response. I then allowed myself the knowledge I knew from my work that dying or grieving does not really change

187

a person. We die or grieve like we live. I was comforted because my dad was always a man of few words. He was confident in his eternal destination and if something needed to be taken care of, he would let us know.

Of all these other losses listed, and more not listed, it is good to acknowledge the pain.

Allow the person to lead. Very few times in life do we have to push another adult, nor do they need us to pull them from ahead. Rather, we need to walk beside people in the ups and downs, the sobs, sniffles, and smiles of life.

 ## QUICK TIPS

- Treat them with compassion and grace like you would if they suffered the loss of a physical death.
- Send cards, invitations, thoughtful gifts to show you are thinking of them.
- Respect boundaries of privacy with information—don't pry for details.
- Offer help with children if you can, so parents can have a break.
- Offer meal support—remember that grieving people need to eat, too, and making food can be a chore.
- Offer financial support if you feel led to do so—help with bills or a small denomination gift card is thoughtful.

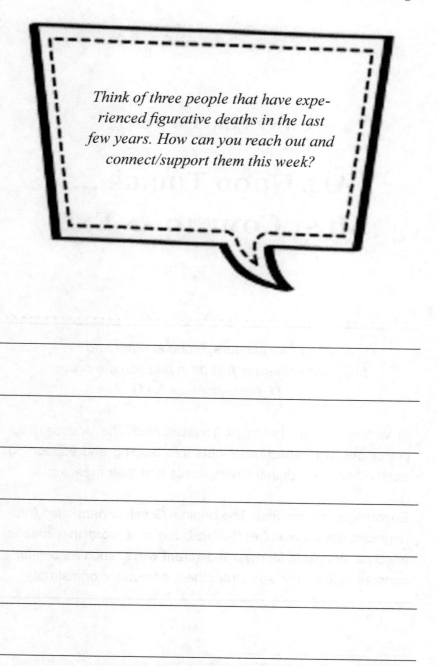

Think of three people that have experienced figurative deaths in the last few years. How can you reach out and connect/support them this week?

CHAPTER TWELVE

ALL GOOD THINGS ... MUST COME TO AN END

· ·

Therefore encourage one another and
build each other up, just as in fact you are doing.
(1 Thessalonians 5:11)

In writing to the church of Thessalonica, the apostle Paul points out two impactful insights into helping and supporting each other. The original Greek words and their meaning:

Encourage one another: The original Greek is *parakaleo* (pro-nounced par-ak-al-eh'-o).[42] *Parakaleo* is a word that means to come alongside in several different ways, such as comfort, console, encourage and strengthen, admonish, or instruct.

· ·

---

[42] Standfordedu. *https://web.stanford.edu/group/parakaleo/about.html#:~:text=%22 Parakaleo%22%20means%20%22to%20call,aspects%20of%20the%20 counseling%20process.*

Build each other up: Here, the Greek is *oioikodomeo* (pronounced oy-kod-om-eh'-o).[43] This word is associated with the construction process, one step of which is laying a foundation.

Building something takes many steps and many skillsets, and it takes time. We can see from this verse that when we put together our gifts, compassion, and hope, we are building up the body of Christ together.

Bethany

A Captain Obvious thought here: the older you get, you will experience more and more people in your life that die or experience serious losses. With each experience, you might gain additional insight about grief and a little more empathy for others going through it. You will get better at reacting to others' needs, and even anticipating what their needs might be, and can be ready to support them. We will make the effort, show up, be there—for the long haul, help to remember and honor their person, say their names ... there are so many ways to support the people we care about. Be intentional, genuine, specific, and consistent. Helping others in their time of need is not only a blessing to them and to you, but it is what we are called to do in our own gifted ways.

God doesn't give us anything just for our own benefit. He wants us to use our talents, skills, and gifts for the benefit of others and build each other up. In 1 Peter 4:10 (NIV), it is declared, "Each of you should use whatever gift you have received to serve others, as faithful stewards of God's grace in its various forms."

---

[43] BibleHub.com https://biblehub.com/greek/3618.htm

As part of our faith journey and with a desire to help those who are grieving, it's possible that we are not using the best gifts that God provided to us. We might do what we think is expected of us instead of what we were made for. We might be relying on societal norms or what our friends do when it might not be using our best gift. For example, based on the title of this book, maybe we weren't meant to provide (another) lasagna to our grieving friend. I'm one of those people who have other gifts; I make a lousy lasagna. (And after so much work, it's discouraging!) I hope in this book you have thought about your gifts, talents, and passions when learning about what grieving people really need. When you unite your gifts with the needs of others, you are truly a blessing to them and God, giving Him the glory for it. Pastor Ryan Kimmel of Peace Church in Middleville, Michigan, states that spiritual gifts are "Supernaturally empowered ability given to each Christian by the will of the Holy Spirit to unite and fully equip the church to live out its mission." He continues, "We can't be the church God's called us (you) to be unless we're all using the gifts God's given us."[44] Instead of feeling like you need to do better and/or do more, use what you already have been given.

Ask God to nudge you and help you use your gifts—He's given them to you, and He wants you to use them, even if you need a little help getting started. Greg Ogden, author of *Discipleship Essentials,* states, "When we operate within our giftedness we are being carried along in a current of love that says, 'You were made for this.'"[45] You were made to be a helper—whatever that looks like for you. No matter how big or small you think your gift of support is, it's important. You already have the desire to help your grieving friend. I am praying that you have learned what a grieving person really needs, God to sustain you during the hard moments

---

[44] Kimmel, "A Church Empowered," https://www.peacechurch.cc/a-church-empowered-you-are-filled/, January 9, 2022. 2:04 and 5:54.

[45] Ogden, *Discipleship Essentials,* p.179.

of support, and the spiritual nudges that will remind you to keep checking on your friend, even years later. You are a blessing. No one said this journey of grief support is easy, but maybe you were made for such a time as this. Thank you for being the hands and feet of Jesus to your grieving friend.

Gwen

Stepping outside our comfort zone can produce great results, keeping two things in mind.

The first is about our uncomfortableness when being around those who are hurting. Most people think that someone with many degrees is better suited for the job. Someone who at least has a master's in psychology, theology, and so forth is our natural thought when it comes to being present with someone who is hurting deeply. We are thinking that, even if we are gifted in an area, an expert is still needed. Yet when people are asked what they want in a counselor, the following qualities are desired: respect, sensitivity, warmth, genuineness, trust, immediacy, humility, patience, hope, humor, and heart. People do not say they want someone with many degrees, or someone who talks in clinical or theological terminology, but rather they seek qualities that lie within the capacity of each human heart. It does not take "an expert" to be trustworthy, genuine, patient—you get the point. I hope this knowledge eases your discomfort, empowers you to step in where needed, step out of your giftedness when required, but, above all, calms you to the point where you realize "you were made for this."

Secondly, being a beacon of hope can be a gift to a grieving person. Bereaved people do not possess much hope amidst their pain and suffering, so we need to loan them ours. As for believers, we can speak the truths of the hope we have in Christ. They need to borrow hope: as much as they need and for as long as it is needed. The gift of loaning hope is to communicate the belief that they can and will heal. Hope is an expectation of a good that is yet to be. As a professional grief worker, I do not say, "Just have hope." I demonstrate it, and you can too by knowing they will not always be in this place. I can stay there with them and have confidence that, after the hard work of grief, healing awaits. Envision that hurting people often feel much like a seed who has been buried in the cold, dark ground, trampled and covered with dirt. With care and support, nurturing, watering, they will grow, come out of the darkness, become stronger, and they themselves may go on to help others. This is the beautiful cycle of care.

 QUICK TIPS

- Pray first.
- Speak hope by using supportive language: "I believe in you," "You are not alone," "You are normal," "Your feelings are valid."
- Recognize where your passions are, what you are good at, where your experience is, and consider how those can help a grieving person.
- You were made uniquely you—wonderfully made—you've got this!

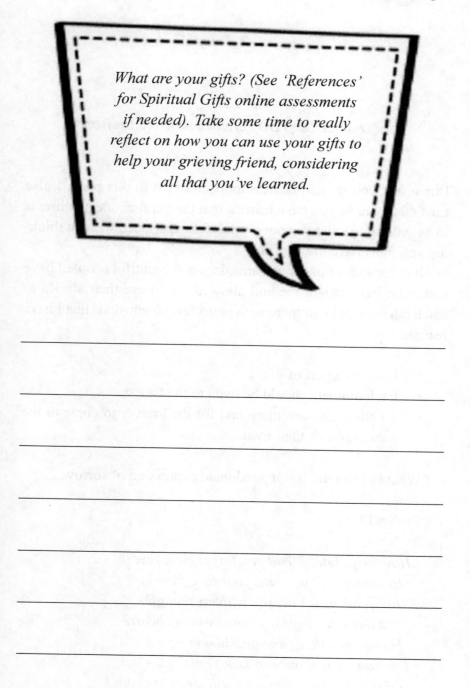

What are your gifts? (See 'References' for Spiritual Gifts online assessments if needed). Take some time to really reflect on how you can use your gifts to help your grieving friend, considering all that you've learned.

_____

_____

_____

_____

_____

_____

Special Note from Gwen about Lament

I trust that you found practical tools and help in this book. I also trust that by now, you have learned that the number one qualifier is to be willing to enter someone's painful experience without thinking you must pave the way out.

It is because of the brave, amazing, and beautiful people I have met, who have taught me and allowed me to use their stories to teach others, that I can share with you a few conclusions that I have learned:

- Death is a part of life.
- Each moment should be lived to the fullest.
- To allow for lamenting and for the griever to come to the conclusion on their own.

What is Lament? It is a passionate expression of sorrow.

Psalm 13

¹ How long, LORD? Will you forget me forever?
How long will you hide your face from me?
2 How long must I wrestle with my thoughts
and day after day have sorrow in my heart?
How long will my enemy triumph over me?
³ Look on me and answer, LORD my God.
Give light to my eyes, or I will sleep in death,

4 and my enemy will say, "I have overcome him,"
and my foes will rejoice when I fall.
⁵ But I trust in your unfailing love;
my heart rejoices in your salvation.
6 I will sing the LORD's praise,
for he has been good to me.

Now, we have talked a lot about feelings in this book. Feelings are normal; feelings are given to us by God; feelings are information. God created them; our feelings are not bad; it is what we do with them that can make them a negative. As we see in this psalm, we can express our lament. As clinicians, we study grief and one theory developed by Stroebe and Schut called "Dual Process Model of Grief," in which we oscillate between two realities: loss-oriented and restoration-oriented.[46] In looking at Psalm 13, in the first four verses, there is a lament in which the author questions God and passionately seeks to ask God how long... "Must I have sorrow in my heart?" (loss-oriented.) This shows us that there is a safe space for lamenting. This is where our friends live when they are hurting. Notice we can come before God as we are, so as friends, please allow for them to not have to pretty up their feelings for you. Lament is as natural an expression as praise. When we are thankful, we give thanks to God. When we have deep pain and distress, we can turn to God in lament.

Then in verses five and six, they come to their "but, yet" conclusion on their own. (Restoration oriented) We as helpers do not have to push them through the pain. We do not have to tell them how to feel; God will reveal that. The pressure is off us. We do not need to pick them up and carry them to the conclusion, but rather stand in the gaps, honoring the bruises and tears. Grieving is hard

---

[46] Margaret Stroebe and Henk Schut, "The Dual Process Model of Coping with Bereavement: Rationale and Description," *Death Studies* 23, no. 3 (1999): 197–224, https://doi.org/10.1080/074811899201046.

work, yet it must be done. For if we rush them through to the light, it is in the darkness that they find God, and we do not want them to miss Him. The beauty of supporting someone through the darkest hour, weeping with those who weep, is when they get to rejoice and we hear them say, "I will sing the Lord's praise, for He has been good to me!"

Restoration at its finest!

ACKNOWLEDGMENTS

Bethany

I cannot thank every person that has been an influence in my healing from grief—there are far too many. I'm grateful to have such support around me—you've kept me standing and persevering so I could write my story to help others. However, to personally thank a few:

My kids: Alek and Lindsey
For the patience you've had with me while I "worked on my computer" and spent time away from you so I could write, I am thankful for you. You both inspire me so much that you are healthy, grateful, happy, and enjoy life. I've tried to be both mom and dad for you, even though that's not fair to anyone. You're learning so young that life's not fair. But it's still good, and so is God. I love you both more than you can ever imagine. You're both my favorite and you are both loved!

My parents: Pat and Sheila
My dad's wise phrase of, "If you fall, you fall (get back up)" carried me. For my mom who willingly spent many weekends at my

house with the kids so I could go away and write without distractions, it was so helpful, appreciated, and necessary to finish this book. Your strength and devotion inspire me. You are both loved!

My "Doing Life Together" Friends
I've vented to you more times than I can count, and you've always listened without judgment, supported me with care, and met me where I was at. You've also laughed at my lame jokes and sarcasm when I needed it the most. When's our next girls' trip? You are all loved!

My Cheerleaders:
Cindy, you have encouraged me from day one to treasure my story and use it to help others. You inspired me to keep going for the right reasons. You've never faded, and the confetti is still abundant years later. YOU are loved!

Tom, I am so grateful for your expert advice, guidance, encouragement, and faith. You are a genuine example of having a servant's heart and loving your family and friends without end. I feel so lucky to get such help from a perfectly seasoned industry leader that's admired by so many. You are loved!

My In-Laws Judy, Phil, Mike, Janet & Willie: My brother Pat, sisters-in-law Nicole and Carolyn, and extended family:
It's not always been easy, but I've felt the love from you and tried to reciprocate the love right back. Despite us all going through grief in our own ways, we've maintained relationships rooted from love. I'm grateful for that and for the relationship you treasure with my kids. You are all loved!

My Friend: Rachel

I prayed that God would bring me a next-door neighbor friend like you, and He delivered in ways that I could have never imagined. You've been there at the happiest and hardest times, and for everything in between. To say you go above and beyond is an understatement. You are loved!

My Backyard Bible Study Friends:

Thank you for joining me and showing up even when life is chaotic. We are admittedly imperfect, but we keep trying year after year. We've supported each other through tremendous struggles, and you've always encouraged me in my writing. You are all loved!

My friend: Jolynn

You're the inspiration for this book. You were determined to truly help me in my greatest time of need, and you wished there were books specifically for the friends of the grieving person so you could understand better how I felt and what I needed. You rushed to and stayed by my side—in both times of tragedy. You're selfless and hilarious. You always call just when I need to feel loved and have a good laugh. You are the real deal. You are loved!

My grieving friends:

So many of you told me your hard stories so that there could be a greater purpose. I appreciate it so much. You are all loved!

My contributing author friend: Gwen:

Thank you for saying, "Yes, I will." God brought us together to collaborate on this important project, and you never gave up on me, even when the finish line seemed so far away. Your wise advice that "(My) story was enough" opened the door to my vulnerability and emotions that I hadn't felt in a long time but made for a more genuine book. I appreciate you sticking by me and contributing in such a powerful way, with a passion to make sure grieving people are well cared for. You are loved!

My Karens: Karen M. and Karen B.
I wouldn't be anywhere without your support, guidance, wisdom, prayers, friendship, and genuine love. You've seen me at my absolute worst, and you helped me in ways I can never repay. You are both loved!

To one of my favorite authors: Bob G.
You personally called me and prayed for me during the hardest time of my life. Years later, we met in person, and you told me I had a story to tell. I hope you will be proud that I got "Undistracted" enough to make it happen. You are loved!

To God:
I owe it all to you. You love me and send helpers to come along side me just when I need it. Everything always turns out! Not often the way I planned it, hoped or prayed for necessarily but the way that is best for me – your will/your way. You are loved and I am yours.

Gwen

My parents:
Emery and Elaine, who were not only the greatest prayer warriors a girl could ever have, but they taught me how to pray about everything. Hence, when I graduated from college, got married, and was seeking my first job, I prayed for the job God had for me. Within moments of that prayer, my grief counselor career was launched. When grief hit my husband and me in years of infertility and babies now in heaven, it was the prayers of my parents that helped me during that time. They did not have to know the details; they just

prayed. I am so thankful for their example and leadership on how to be a Christ-follower.

My husband:
Mike. Life with you has been such an adventure. Although my job contributed to the knowledge that life is short, it has always been you who lived that way and made time for frog-catching, tolerance of others, and listening to children and their stories is a must, especially around the glow of a campfire. Your support of me staying home when our children were little and keeping my feet in grief work was a treasure! I can always count on you for honest input and even though I did not always receive it well, I do appreciate it. You are a steady provider and a great friend, and I thank God for you every day! I love you!

My children:
Travis, Megan, and Rachel. The greatest joy of my life has been being your mother. And now being a mother-in-law to your amazing spouses, Allison and Joey. I am sure I was overly protective at times, an occupational hazard from all the stories I heard. I also know you had to listen to many of those stories when we saw my clients out in public, and they stopped to share with me; you were always so gracious to them. I am forever grateful for the technical support you provide me and for being the first people to share my posts or tell a friend about the work I do. You are the best cheerleaders. I love you all, equally. I know you try to claim the number one spot, but it belongs to all of you!

My siblings:
Cheri and Scott. I feel like this will sound so cliche, but you truly are the best. I cannot imagine two better people to do life with. Even though we have not lived our adult lives in the same state, I feel so connected to you and supported by you and know that I can

trust you with my life! Your willingness to travel for life events, the ease with which we make decisions together, and how you care for our parents have made for a team that could rival any sibling group (even compared to you know who). It is my prayer that our old age brings us time to sit on a porch, drink watered-down Sprite, and share stories about the good old days. I love you both.

To my mother-in-law:
Judie. Where do I even start? You have contributed so much to me as a person, a wife, and a mother. Your endless support for all that I do has been priceless. The help with the kids, the cooking, and the housework when I was working had so many people jealous of my awesome mother-in-law! The way you have handled eighteen years of widowhood has been an inspiration to me and has taught me so much. You are loved.

To my three J's, my jewels:
Jenny, Jodi, and Jodi. There has never been, or ever will be, anyone who makes my soul laugh more than the three of you. Nor will anyone know the secrets that we share. What we share is rare and valuable ... a deep history, a fierce sisterhood, and an unimaginable amount of time in TJ Maxx. Throughout the years, we have supported each other in many good and tough times, some of which could have broken us, but our hearts are connected and for that, I am eternally grateful.

To Wendy, Connie, Sadie, Rachael, and Laura:
You are all special in your own way and have added so much to my life. There is a richness I have that was given to me in the friendship that we share. I can always count on you to listen, support, and advise me. No matter how much time has passed, it is like we were never apart. I just love it when your name comes up on my phone or the fact that I can call you about anything. You have each

contributed to this book with the wisdom you have shared with me. Thank you for being my cheerleader and friend. I love you all.

To my author friend Bethany:
How can I ever thank you enough for inviting me into your story? This opportunity to share some of what I have learned with you and your readers has been so sweet and special. I have loved how right from the start, your heart wanted to help others. You could have just lived life without ever sharing your wisdom and what you have learned, but I am so glad you didn't, and our readers will be so glad too. You are truly a blessing!

To the countless brave bereaved:
I think of you often. I am so grateful for your trust. I am so honored to bear witness to your heartache. It has been a holy space to be invited into your house of pain. You have made me really good at my job; you have added to the richness of my life; and you have taught me what it means to be brave. You get up each day and face it, knowing there is more pain in today, yet you go on. You do the hard work of grief. You cry yourself to sleep each night yet wake each day ready to survive another day. I salute you. You really are strong; you really can endure. You are my inspiration to encourage others. I treasure you; without you, this book would not have been. Thank you.

There are countless others who have added to my life and this book. You have been in my life as a coworker, neighbor, friend, Bible study, or life group member. You have listened to my stories, prayed with me or for me, and have made an impact on me. I am grateful and I thank God at every remembrance of you!

NOTES

RESOURCES:
HELPFUL TOOLS TO OFFER TO
YOUR GRIEVING FRIEND

Author recommended children's books:

- *Sam's Dad Died: A Child's Book of Hope Through Grief* by Margaret M. Holmes. Centering Corporation 1999.
- *Lifetimes: The Beautiful Way to Explain Death to Children* by Bryan Mellonie. Bantam 2009.
- *When I'm feeling Sad* by Trace Moroney. School Specialty Publishing 2006.
- *Helping Me Say Goodbye* by Janice Silverman. Fairview Press 1999.
- *Saying Goodbye to Daddy* by Judtih Vigna Albert. Witman and Company 1991.
- *What Is Heaven Like* by Pamela Querin. Bethany House 2006.
- *When Families Grieve.* Sesame Workshop https://sesamestreetincommunities.org/topics/grief/
- *A Hug from Heaven* by Anna Whiston-Donaldson. Mascot Books 2018.

Author recommended books for the grieving person:

- *Traveling Through Grief* by Susan Zonnebelt-Smeenge & Robert Devries.
- *Healthy Healing: A Guide to Working Out Grief* by Michelle Steinke-Baumgard.
- *I Wasn't Ready to Say Goodbye* by Brook Noel and Pamela D. Blair, PhD. Sourcebooks Inc 2000.
- *Companion Through the Darkness: Inner Dialogues on Grief* by Stephanie Ericsson. Harper Collins 1993.
- *Rare Bird, A Memoir of Loss and Love* (Child-loss) by Anna Whiston-Donaldson. Convergent Books 2015.
- *Dancing on my Ashes: Learning to Love the One Who Gives and Takes Away* by Heather Filion and Holly Snell. Tate Publishing 2010.
- *Choosing to See, by Mary Beth Chapman. Revell 2011*
- *When God Doesn't Fix it, by Laura Story. W Publishing Group, 2016.*

Author recommended programs for Grief Recovery:

- Griefshare.org
- Grief-Guide.com
- A Life after Breath experience: (Widow retreat) Mattersoflifeandbreath.com

Author recommended grief programs for children:

- Camps and support centers can be located at Childrengrieve.org (National Alliance for Children's Grief)

Podcast:

- *Always Andy's Mom* (interviews bereaved moms. Andysmom.com)
- *Scattering Hope* (Specific to suicide loss)

Websites

- Onefitwidow.com (Grief recovery & inspiration through fitness, education, and adventure)
- Speakupforhope.org (Hope and Healing for inmates and their families)

Gifts/Honorary:

- Backpocketdesign.com
- LivingThreadsMinistry.org
- AngelsofGrace.com

Spiritual Gifts Assessment Links:

- Truewiring.com/gifts/
- Spritualgiftstest.com

The above-referenced resources are ones that we (Bethany and/or Gwen) have had personal experience with and recommend. We are not compensated for listing their resources here. For additional resources please feel free to reach out to us at Gwen@grief-guide. com or Bethany@bethanyfrance.com.

ABOUT THE AUTHORS

Bethany lives in West Michigan with her two kids, one sneaky/naughty cat (Leo), one fat/cuddly cat (Lucy) and a rambunctious, but faithful lab named Scout. She loves her family, friends, church and predictable romantic comedy movies. Her "dad" jokes and love of puns and use of sweet sarcasm is an attempt to lighten the moods around her and make people smile. Bethany works full time in the field of Human Resources where she uses her education (MBA/SHRM-CP) and experience to resolve conflicts in the workplace but with grace and empathy at what employees might be going through. Bethany has a devotional story published within "And Then There was Light" – EA Publishing – and maintains a blog at bethanyfranceblog.com focused on Faith, Family, Friends and Giving Hope to the Grieving. You can also find her at Bethany France, Writer on Facebook.

Gwen is a licensed social worker in the state of Michigan and holds a certification in thanatology, the study of death, dying, and bereavement. She has spent her entire career around grief and loss, spanning from hospice care, funeral home aftercare support, and as executive director at a West Michigan grief support ministry. She is the co-author of *Mourning Star,* a Christ-centered grief curriculum for children, teens, and adults. She knows what grief feels like for her, but most of her experiences come from walking alongside thousands of bereaved individuals who bravely taught her about grief. She is a wife, mother of three adult children (recently promoted to grandmother!), and lives in Portland, Michigan. She is active in her church and volunteers frequently. Gwen is the owner of Your Grief Guide. Through online classes, virtual checkpoints, and educational presentations to those who are grieving and supporting bereaved friends and family, she aims to normalize the reactions to loss, give practical guidance, and provide hope for healing. She is a national speaker, featuring topics on grief and loss, including those affected by suicide, conducts programs to healthcare, corporate training, schools, and churches. You can find her at Gwen@ grief-guide.com, FB grief-guide, and Instagram at: gwenkapcia, or the website, grief-guide.com.

By Lindsey France

ABOUT THE TITLE:
NOT ANOTHER LASAGNA

We thought of this title from almost the beginning of the project and got great feedback that it was a catchy, memorable title. However, an experience that Gwen had solidified our desire to keep it as the title.

I, Gwen, was speaking at an event that was designed for family and friends whose person died by suicide. One young woman who was attending had been asked beforehand to sit on a panel during the event as she had suffered the death of her brother by suicide and could offer her advice and testimony about her experience. She had made notes in her journal about what she might offer during her panel discussion.

When I finished my speaking portion, which included talking about this book by name, that it was in progress, and I hoped that it would help to improve support for those that are grieving. After the event, several attendees approached me to talk about their experiences and were thankful that I was there to speak. The young lady from the panel talked to me as well and told me that she got chills when the title of this book was mentioned. She opened her journal, showed me what she had written the night before, and said that we had chosen a great title for the book.

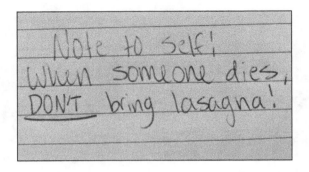

Photo credit Mackenzie R., in memory of Zach Ford (9/22/03-12/5/19)

Printed in the USA
CPSIA information can be obtained
at www.ICGtesting.com
LVHW022126180524
780462LV00011B/425

9 798990 436237